# LOG CABINS AND OUTBUILDINGS

# LOG CABINS AND OUTBUILDINGS

## A Guide to Building Homes, Barns, Greenhouses, and More

By the United States Department of Agriculture

Skyhorse Publishing

Visit our website at www.skyhorsepublishing.com.

10 9 8 7 6 5 4

Library of Congress Cataloging-in-Publication Data is available on file.

Cover design by Michael Short
Cover photo credit: iStockphoto

Print ISBN: 978-1-5107-3981-9
Ebook ISBN: 978-1-5107-3982-6

Printed in China

# CONTENTS

|  | Plan No. | Page |
|---|---|---|
| Introduction | | 1 |
| Cabins | | 2 |
|     Vacation cabin for two | 5184 | 2 |
|     Three-room cabin | 5185 | 3 |
|     Vacation cabin for four | 5186 | 4 |
|     Cabin | 5928 | 5 |
|     Cabin, masonry construction | 5968 | 6 |
|     Cabin with dormitory loft | 6013 | 9 |
|     A-frame cabins | 5964 | 11 |
| | 5965 | 11 |
|     A-frame cabin | 6003 | 15 |
|     Log cabin | 5506 | 17 |
|     Log cabin | 5507 | 18 |
|     Log cabin | 7013 | 18 |
|     Pole-frame cabin | 6002 | 20 |
|     Pole-frame cabin | 6004 | 22 |
|     Vacation house, frame construction | 5997 | 24 |
|     Tenant house | 7010 | 27 |
|     Farm cottage | 7137 | 28 |
|     Adirondack-type shelter | 5998 | 30 |
| Barns and Equipment for Horses | | 32 |
|     Expansible barn for riding horses | 5838 | 32 |
|     Two-horse trailer | 5943 | 33 |
|     Saddle horse barn | 5994 | 35 |
|     Eight-stall horse barn | 6010 | 36 |
|     Seventeen-stall horse barn | 6011 | 38 |
|     One-and-a-half-story horse barn | 6024 | 40 |
|     Portable stable for a horse | 6082 | 42 |
|     Horse equipment | 6014 | 44 |
|     Horse show rings | 6015 | 46 |
| Greenhouses | | 48 |
|     Plastic-covered greenhouse | 5941 | 48 |
|     Plastic-covered greenhouse | 5946 | 50 |
|     Greenhouse framing for plastic covering | 6029 | 52 |
|     Hotbed and propagating frame | 5971 | 54 |
|     Mini-hotbed and propagating frame | 6080 | 57 |
| Recreation Facilities | | 59 |
|     Outdoor fireplace | 5188 | 59 |
|     Boat landing | 5975 | 61 |
|     Picnic shelter of wood construction | 5995 | 62 |
|     Concrete block incinerator | 5996 | 64 |
|     Sheltered barbeque pits | 6020 | 66 |
| | 6022 | 66 |
|     Recreational pavilion with kitchen | 6079 | 68 |
|     Comfort station for campgrounds | 6083 | 70 |
|     Storage sheds | 6086 | 72 |
| | 6093 | 72 |
|     Utility sheds | 6100 | 73 |

# RECREATIONAL BUILDINGS AND FACILITIES

*Agricultural Research Service*

# INTRODUCTION

This illustrated list of currently available building plans was compiled by the Cooperative Farm Building Plan Exchange. The plans were developed by the cooperative effort of Extension Service (USDA). State Extension Service, State Experiment Stations, Cooperative State Research Service (USDA), and Agricultural Engineering Research Division, Agricultural Research Service (USDA).

The building plans, their purpose, and some of the construction details are shown in the illustrations and are described in the brief text for each plan.

Economy of material and labor has been given particular emphasis. The structures are efficient and useful for the purposes intended.

Complete working drawings of the plans may be obtained from the extension agricultural engineer at your State university. There may be a small charge to cover cost of printing. If you do not know the location of your State university, send your request to Agricultural Engineer, Extension Service, U.S. Department of Agriculture, Washington, D.C. 20250. He will forward your request to the correct university.

# CABINS

## VACATION CABIN FOR TWO, PLAN NO. 5184

This low cost, one-room cabin may be set on pressure-treated post foundations to reduce construction costs. Where termites are a problem, the floor can be made of concrete, or if wood is used in such areas, joists and sills should be chemically treated.

Barn boards of random widths and half-round battens can be used for the exterior wall covering and can be painted. Other details of construction are shown on the illustrations.

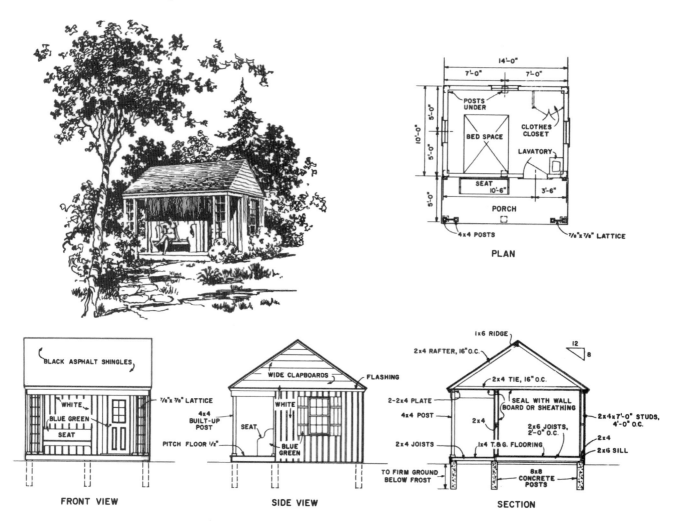

# THREE-ROOM CABIN, PLAN NO. 5185

This cabin is suitable for camping or could be utilized as a bunkhouse during the harvest season. It could also serve temporarily as living quarters for a family while a permanent farmhouse was being built. The cookstove would furnish heat. In cold climates the cabin should be insulated.

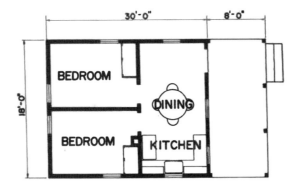

# VACATION CABIN FOR FOUR, PLAN NO. 5186

This economical building provides for Pullman-type berths. If a central heat source is not practical, a chimney should be added to provide for a heater. Space is also provided for a toilet as shown on the plan.

The sill is steel-strapped to concrete posts that extend below frost line.

Floor joists are framed into the sill and securely anchored with metal fasteners.

Both floor joists and sill should be protected from termite attack.

This building is frame construction with the exterior surface covered with rough-sawn, random width boards and 1¼-inch, half-round, wood battens.

Interior has tongue-and-groove flooring, with walls and ceiling covered with building board or sheathing.

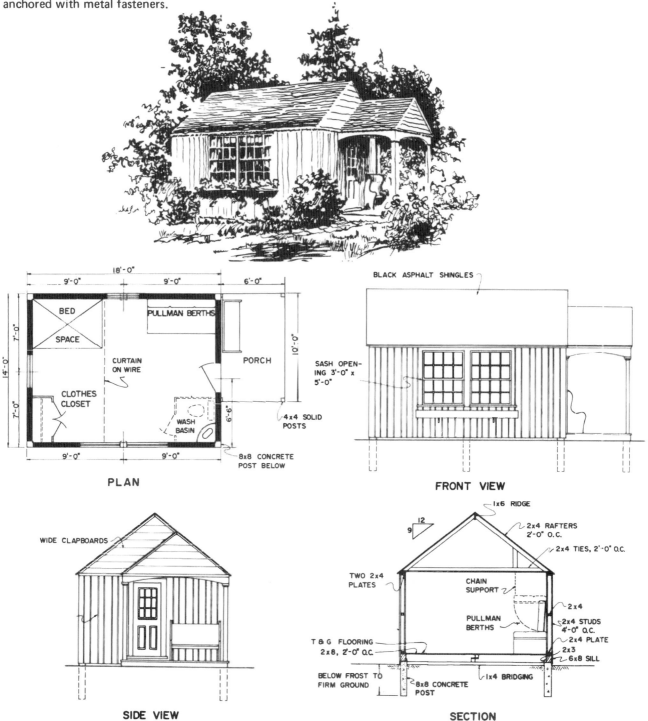

PLAN

FRONT VIEW

SIDE VIEW

SECTION

4

## CABIN, PLAN NO. 5928

The basic floor plan for this frame cabin is 24 by 24 feet, slab-on-grade construction. The exterior shell can be built and the plumbing roughed in at a reasonably low cost. Interior finish, storage walls, and an addition can be added later.

The simple interior arrangement is flexible and can be adapted to many uses—a beach house, lake or mountain cabin; a low-cost permanent home with one, two, or three bedrooms; or a temporary home. The outside may be rustic or of the finest modern siding. The inside may have rough framing and concrete floor exposed, or it may be highly finished. Thus, the design fits a wide variety of needs.

## Alternate floor plans

The alternate plans of this cabin can be utilized for additional income from a developed recreational area. The basic building can be arranged in several ways, depending on the type of facility and on accommodations needed by vacationers. For example, a screened porch, a bunk room, or two additional bedrooms can be added.

The working drawings show construction details for storage walls—2 feet wide, 4 feet long, and 8 feet high—which may be built from standard 4- by 8-foot sheets of material. The roof trusses eliminate any need for interior load-bearing walls, so the walls may be located wherever desired. If built lower than ceiling height, they can be moved easily.

If the cabin is to be used as a permanent dwelling, storage space is needed outside. The space should be large enough to accommodate paints, hand and garden tools, lawn mower, outboard motor, gasoline, and similar equipment and supplies. Also, the shed should be large enough to permit handyman activities.

Careful consideration should be given to the heating system. If expansion is planned, the system must be capable of heating the larger unit.

The alternate plan shows one arrangement that is possible for expansion. It has more living, sleeping, and storage space than the basic plan, but it also requires outdoor storage for a permanent type home. The working drawings show only the expanded building with storage walls.

The roof trusses used in the design are simple lap-nailed construction and have been load tested. The truss members can be nailed together and trimmed later to eliminate precision marking and cutting. If the details of the working drawings are followed, a reliable roof support can be easily and quickly constructed.

# CABIN, MASONRY CONSTRUCTION, PLAN NO. 5968

Concrete masonry construction is suggested for this modern cabin because concrete is low cost, durable, easy to maintain, and attractive.

Complete kitchen facilities in the cabin combine with the living-dining area to form a unified activities center for the family. Though the basic plan calls for one bedroom, the activities center is large enough for a family that would need three bedrooms. The two extra bedrooms may be added at the rear, as suggested in the working drawings, without alteration of the present rooms or equipment. A bath with shower, a space for a washer, and good storage facilities contribute to pleasant and convenient living in this cabin.

Suggestions for block selection, insulation, finishing materials, and paint are given below. These ideas, along with personal preference for trim and for paint color combinations, can be used to give warmth and character to the cabin. Further help and suggestions are available from the Portland Cement Association, which cooperated in the development of this plan.

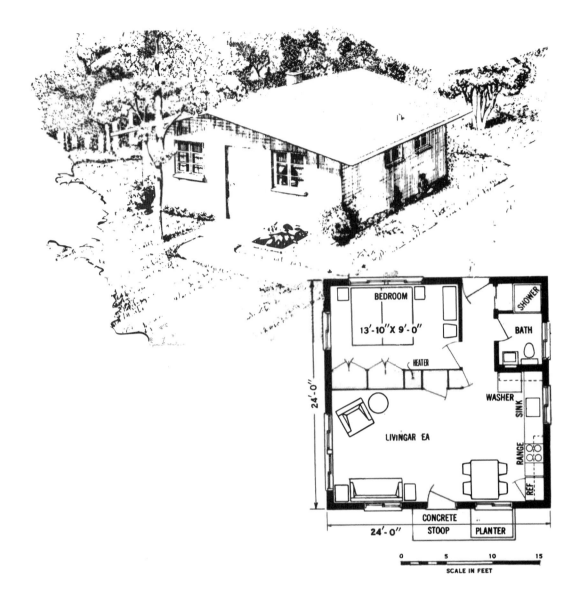

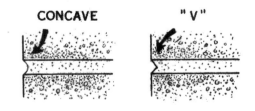

## Block selection

The working drawings show 4- by 8- by 16-inch concrete block units, which give horizontal mortar lines at 4-inch intervals. These relatively close-spaced mortar joints have a pleasing appearance, but the finished cost is increased by one-third as compared with that of standard 8- by 8- by 16-inch units.

Properly tooled joints are very important for watertight walls and for overall good appearance. Concave or "v" joints are recommended.

When mortar in joints is "thumb print" hard, it should be firmly pressed into the concave or "v"

formation with a tooling device that is wider than the joint and 24 to 36 inches long. This long tooling device makes straight, uniform horizontal joints.

## Insulation

Insulation above the ceiling is recommended for cabins built in any climate and for use in any season. Either loose fill or batt-type insulation may be used. Vermiculite fill in the cores of the blocks and foamed semirigid insulation about the perimeter of the floor slab are necessary for winter comfort. Lightweight-aggregate blocks are recommended because insulation is easier to apply to them than to the denser concrete blocks with sand and gravel aggregate. Lightweight blocks are also easier to handle, and nails can be driven into them.

## Finishing material

Interior-wall, ceiling, and floor finishes can be applied before partitions are erected. This saves cutting and fitting labor. Ceiling tiles made of insulating board are popular for this type of building because no further finishing is required. Low-cost asphalt tiles serve well over a concrete floor slab.

A latex paint is recommended for the interior walls. Besides being economical and easy to apply, it is well suited for masonry and the other inside materials. The exterior masonry walls should have a base coat of portland cement paint (a special cement powder to be mixed with water) for watertightness. Apply this with a stiff-bristle scrub brush to fill the pores of the block. The second exterior coat should be an acrylic resin, outside latex paint.

## Interior partitions

The clear span of the roof trusses permits free placement of interior partitions. If the partitions are not hindered by wiring or plumbing, they can be easily moved for remodeling. Partitions should be slightly less than ceiling height and wedged at the bottom to press them against the ceiling.

The working drawings show construction details of the storage room wall that separates the living area from the bedroom. Built from standard 4- by 8-foot sheets of material, the wall is 2 feet deep by 8 feet high.

Perforated hardboard is suggested for closet doors and backs, for ventilation as well as for its decorative quality. Brackets and hooks can be placed in the perforated board to make the storage space more usable.

Construction of the heater enclosure will depend on the type of heating unit to be installed.

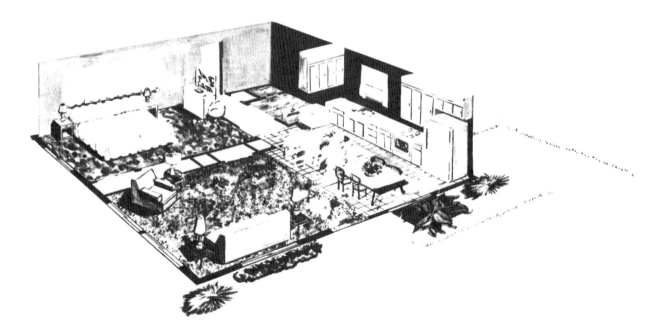

# CABIN WITH DORMITORY LOFT, PLAN NO. 6013

1 ST FLOOR .. 22' X 24'

LOFT ........ 12' X 24'

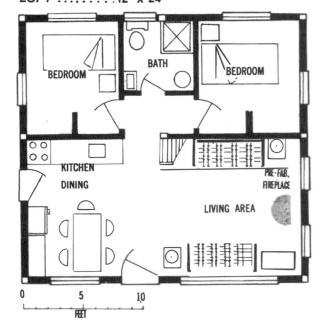

This one-and-a-half-story cabin has two bedrooms and a loft sleeping area. The loft is over the first floor bedrooms and has clearances of 7 feet at the ridge beam and 3 feet at the outside wall.

An open-type ceiling gives a feeling of spaciousness to the kitchen and living area and cuts construction costs. A prefabricated fireplace is suggested on the plan.

Pole framing helps to make construction easy for the less-experienced builder and eliminates the need for expensive masonry foundations. A woodframe floor is used in the structure shown and is most suitable for a sloping site. A concrete floor would be more economical when the house is built on a well-drained, level site. A pole-supported deck is suggested for more indoor-outdoor relaxation space.

Rough-sawn native material is used wherever possible. The choice of interior finishing material is left to the builder. Slight changes in the wall framing could be made if insulation and interior finish are to be added.

# construction details

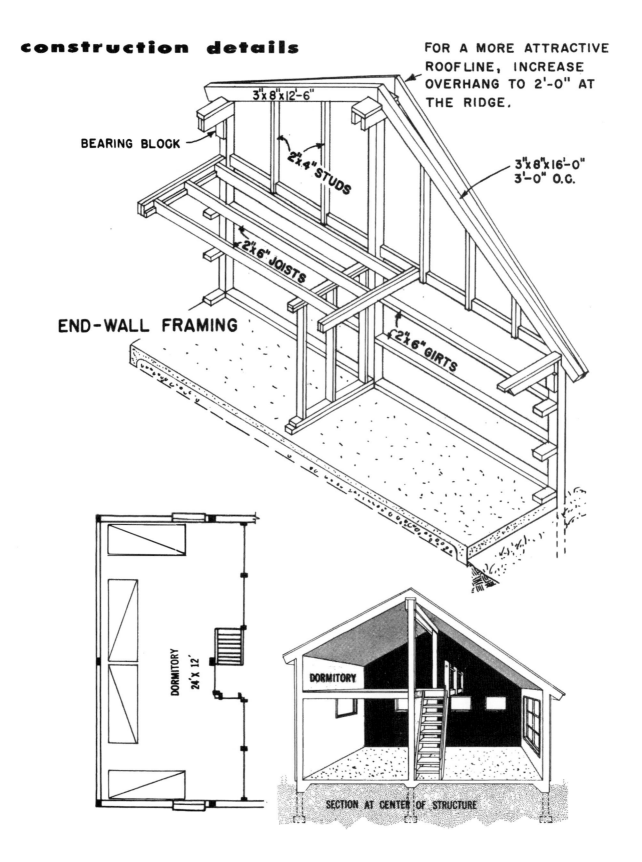

3"x8"x12'-6"

FOR A MORE ATTRACTIVE ROOFLINE, INCREASE OVERHANG TO 2'-0" AT THE RIDGE.

BEARING BLOCK

2"x4" STUDS

3"x8"x16'-0"
3'-0" O.C.

2"x6" JOISTS

END-WALL FRAMING

2"x6" GIRTS

DORMITORY
24' X 12'

DORMITORY

SECTION AT CENTER OF STRUCTURE

# A-FRAME CABINS, PLANS NO. 5964 AND NO. 5965

These two cabins (24-foot and 36-foot A-frames) are designed for recreational purposes in mountain areas or at a beach. They can be built by three or four people who have reasonable ability in the use of tools. Someone with a knowledge of concrete work may be required to place the footings. The frame itself should present no problems; nor should erection of the end walls, roof, and interior partitions. It is assumed that electricity will be available at the site to permit the use of power tools and to provide for lighting, heating, and cooking.

Each cabin is provided with a modern kitchen that contains a refrigerator, range, sink, and adequate cabinet space. Provision is made for a water heater under one corner of the floor cabinet arrangement. The bathroom contains a lavatory, toilet, and shower. A storage locker for linens is provided in the bathroom. The water supply would probably come from a well or spring; and the piping, where exposed to the outside air should be properly insulated and provided with drain valves so that all water can be drained from the system when the cabin is not occupied during winter weather.

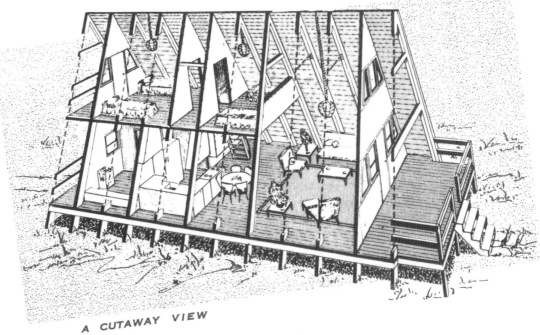

A CUTAWAY VIEW

## Plan No. 5965

The 36-foot cabin contains three bedrooms, one on the first floor and two on the second floor. The front bedroom on the second floor is a balcony that overlooks the two-story living room. If sleeping space for more than six persons is required, cots can be placed in the living room.

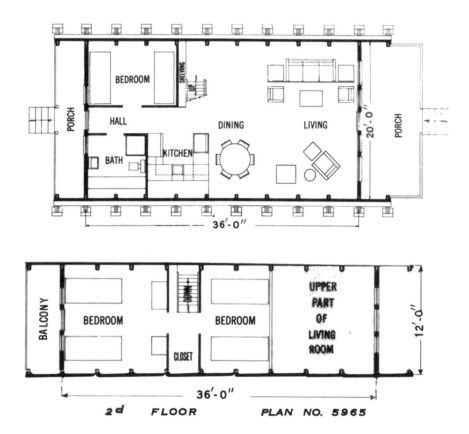

## Plan No. 5964

The 24-foot cabin contains two bedrooms, both on the second floor. The living-dining area is smaller than that in the 36-foot cabin. The living room is only one story high.

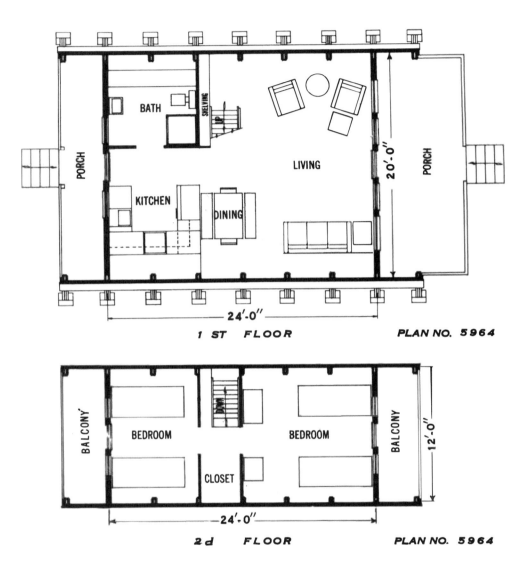

1 ST FLOOR      PLAN NO. 5964

2d FLOOR      PLAN NO. 5964

## Other features in both cabins

Ventilation in both cabins is good; the windows at each end provide excellent circulation of air.

Storage shelving is indicated adjacent to the ship's ladder that leads to the second floor.

If a fireplace is desired, a prefabricated unit may be installed. Wood may be stored under the cabin for use during winter or for cooking.

The working drawings of the smaller cabin show that the size of the rear bedroom can be increased by extending the second floor to include the rear balcony. The second floor can also be extended at the front of the cabin if desired. If this is done, the door shown on the plan should be replaced by a double-hung window.

# View of section

This section gives some ideas for constructing the A-frame. After the footings have been placed, the lower half of the frame may be erected and the rough flooring nailed in place at the first- and second-floor levels. The second floor can be used as a work platform while the upper half of the frame is put in place. The roof sheathing should then be put on, followed by the finished roofing. The end walls may then be framed and completed and, finally, the interior partitions.

For added protection in cold climates the space under the first floor and in the end walls should be insulated. Additional insulation may be installed on the underside of the roof sheathing between the frames if the climate requires.

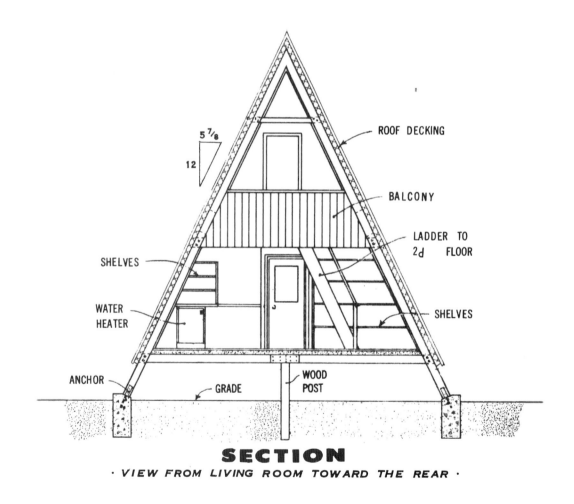

## SECTION
· VIEW FROM LIVING ROOM TOWARD THE REAR ·

# A-FRAME CABIN, PLAN NO. 6003

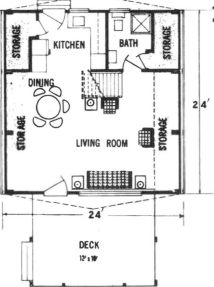

The 24- by 24-foot A-frame cabin, a recreational second home that is popular throughout the United States, has been built in mountain areas, at the shore from Maine to Florida, and across the country. Like the traditional cabins, this A-frame cabin provides quite comfortable living space for a family of four or five. Sleeping space for weekend visitors can be provided easily by rearranging the furniture in the large bedroom on the second floor.

The first floor of the cabin contains a living-dining room, a compact kitchen, a bathroom with shower, and adequate storage space. The living-dining room runs the full width of the building, with storage space on each side.

491-229 O - 73 - 3

The locale and climatic conditions are major factors for the builder to consider when deciding if a heating system and insulation are needed.

The kitchen at the rear of the cabin contains space for a sink, a refrigerator, a range, and base and wall cabinets. A ship's ladder stairway leads to the second floor, and a dormer-type window extension in the roof adds light and ventilation to this area.

With some knowledge of carpentry and the ability to use ordinary hand tools, three or four men should have no serious problems building this cabin. Care should be taken in locating and setting the pressure-treated posts. The A-frames should be assembled flat on the ground, raised into position, and braced until the flooring is put in place. The roof sheathing should be placed, the ends cut to the shape of the overhang, then the roofing applied. The end walls and partitions may easily be installed and the kitchen and bathroom fixtures placed. Redwood or cypress lumber siding will take on a weathered finish and eliminate the need for periodic painting.

# CONSTRUCTION NOTES:

Use rough lumber for all structural framing. Lap rough, 1-inch boards for end-wall siding. Other materials or methods may be substituted.

Rafters and floor beams are 24-feet long to facilitate construction of the A-frame on the ground. If some saving in intial cost is necessary, add the deck in the front later. Interior finish is left to builder's choice.

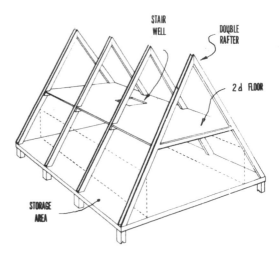

FRAMING DIAGRAM

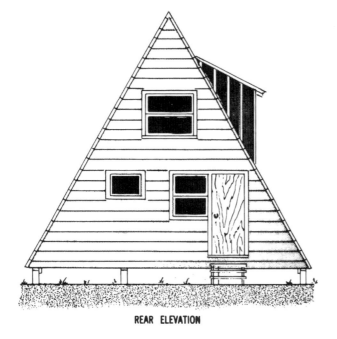

REAR ELEVATION

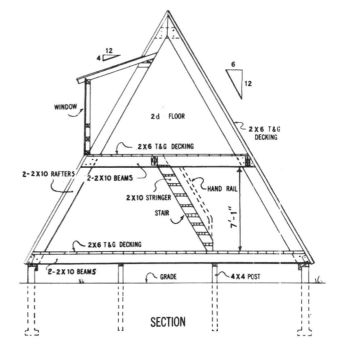

SECTION

# LOG CABIN, PLAN NO. 5506

This five-room cabin, designed principally for camping, would make a fairly comfortable house for a small family. A basement could be provided, with the entrance down a stairway from the back proch. Loft space could be reached from an open stair in the living room.

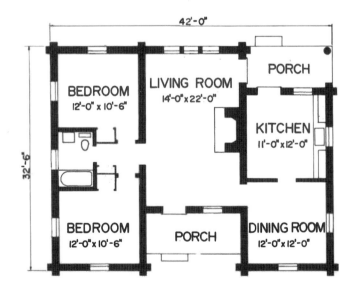

# LOG CABIN, PLAN NO. 5507

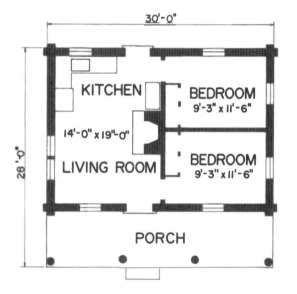

KITCHEN

BEDROOM
9'-3" x 11'-6"

14'-0" x 19'-0"

LIVING ROOM

BEDROOM
9'-3" x 11'-6"

30'-0"

28'-0"

PORCH

This three-room log cabin would be especially appropriate for a camp in the woods or on the lakeshore. The back of the fireplace in the living room gives heat to the bedrooms. The large porch is especially desirable if the house is to be used as a summer home. Porch posts of peeled logs are appropriate for this cabin.

# LOG CABIN, PLAN NO. 7013

In a well-wooded region, this rustic log cabin would be suitable for a small family starting farm life. Or, it might be used as a tenant house or a summer cottage. The grouping of doors and windows reduces the work that usually goes into log construction and provides good cross ventilation. The single, main bearing partition and other partitions are easily framed. A circulator heater, large living-room fireplace, and the wood or coal kitchen range furnish heat.

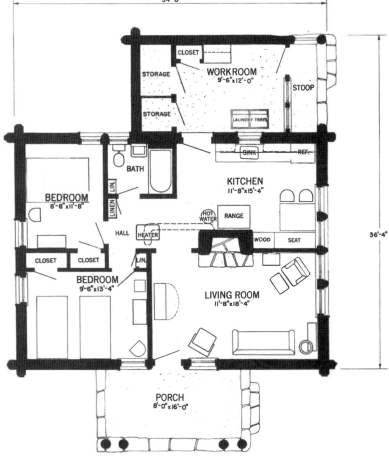

**FLOOR PLAN**

Within the floor plan:

- 34'-0"
- CLOSET
- STORAGE
- WORKROOM 9'-6"x12'-0"
- STOOP
- STORAGE
- LAUNDRY TRAYS
- SINK
- REF.
- BATH
- LINEN
- KITCHEN 11'-8"x15'-4"
- BEDROOM 8'-8"x11'-8"
- HOT WATER
- RANGE
- 36'-4"
- HALL
- HEATER
- WOOD
- SEAT
- CLOSET
- CLOSET
- LIN.
- BEDROOM 9'-6"x13'-4"
- LIVING ROOM 11'-8"x18'-4"
- PORCH 8'-0"x16'-0"

# POLE-FRAME CABIN, PLAN NO. 6002

**24' x 24'**

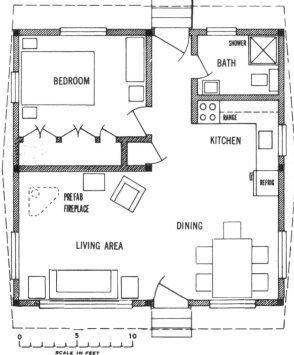

SHOWER

BATH

BEDROOM

RANGE

KITCHEN

REFRIG

PREFAB FIREPLACE

DINING

LIVING AREA

0    5    10

SCALE IN FEET

This one-bedroom structure, simply designed for comfort and economy, can be used as a vacation retreat or campsite. It features low-cost pole-frame construction, design simplicity, and flexibility of arrangement.

The use of poles permits rapid erection, minimum site preparation, and decreased foundation expenses. The poles also serve as the wall framework to which other members are fastened. The life expectancy of a pole-frame structure, with the commercial preservative-treating processes in use today, can be as long as 75 years. The structure can be made very attractive both inside and out, depending on materials available, taste, and cost.

Rough-sawn, native lumber is used in the board-and-batten siding. Several kinds of material are available for use as coverings.

Location and type of window treatment is flexible.

With a kitchen and bath suggested, the interior is efficiently arranged for pleasant living. A prefabricated fireplace could be installed, if necessary.

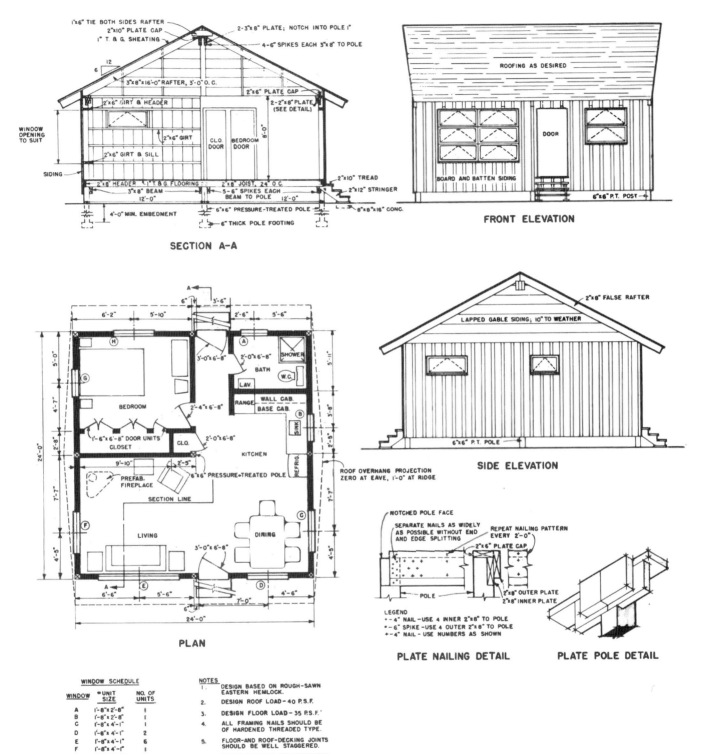

SECTION A-A

FRONT ELEVATION

SIDE ELEVATION

PLAN

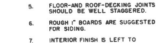

PLATE NAILING DETAIL

PLATE POLE DETAIL

LEGEND
+ – 4" NAIL – USE 4 INNER 2"x8" TO POLE
• – 6" SPIKE – USE 4 OUTER 2"x8" TO POLE
+ – 4" NAIL – USE NUMBERS AS SHOWN

| WINDOW SCHEDULE | | |
|---|---|---|
| WINDOW | *UNIT SIZE | NO. OF UNITS |
| A | 1'-8"x 2'-8" | 1 |
| B | 1'-8"x 2'-8" | 1 |
| C | 1'-8"x 4'-1" | 1 |
| D | 1'-8"x 4'-1" | 2 |
| E | 1'-8"x 4'-1" | 6 |
| F | 1'-8"x 4'-1" | 1 |
| G | 1'-8"x 2'-8" | 1 |
| H | 1'-8"x 4'-1" | 1 |

* ALL AWNING WINDOW UNIT SIZES ARE APPROXIMATE. OTHER WINDOW SIZES AND/OR STYLES SUBSTITUTED AS DESIRED.

NOTES
1. DESIGN BASED ON ROUGH-SAWN EASTERN HEMLOCK.
2. DESIGN ROOF LOAD – 40 P.S.F.
3. DESIGN FLOOR LOAD – 35 P.S.F.
4. ALL FRAMING NAILS SHOULD BE OF HARDENED THREADED TYPE.
5. FLOOR-AND ROOF-DECKING JOINTS SHOULD BE WELL STAGGERED.
6. ROUGH 1" BOARDS ARE SUGGESTED FOR SIDING.
7. INTERIOR FINISH IS LEFT TO BUILDERS DISCRETION.

BASED ON UNIV. OF MASS. PLAN MC-4613

# POLE-FRAME CABIN, PLAN NO. 6004

This structure was designed for builders having limited finances, time, and construction skills. Besides being used as campsite living quarters, it can be an auxiliary structure for such other uses as a concession stand or a storage shelter.

The use of pole framing is in keeping with the objectives of design simplicity, low cost, and flexibility

of arrangement. Pole framing is not necessarily unattractive from either the exterior or the interior. Several kinds of covering materials can be used, depending on cost, desired appearance, and availability of the material. This plan suggests using rough-sawn board-and-batten siding with 10- to 12-inch-wide boards and 2- to 3-inch-wide battens over cracks between the boards. Such siding is economical, attractive, and easily applied.

Though a wood-framed floor structure on a level site is shown here, this type of construction is also adaptable to a sloping site. A concrete floor slab could be substituted on a well-drained, level site.

The window treatment is quite flexible as to type and location.

THE FLOOR PLAN IS 16 FEET BY 20 FEET WITH SIDE-WALL POLES SPACED 10 FEET ON CENTER. THE STRUCTURE CAN BE EXTENDED TO 30 FEET THEREBY ALLOWING ONE END TO BE PARTITIONED INTO SLEEPING AREAS.

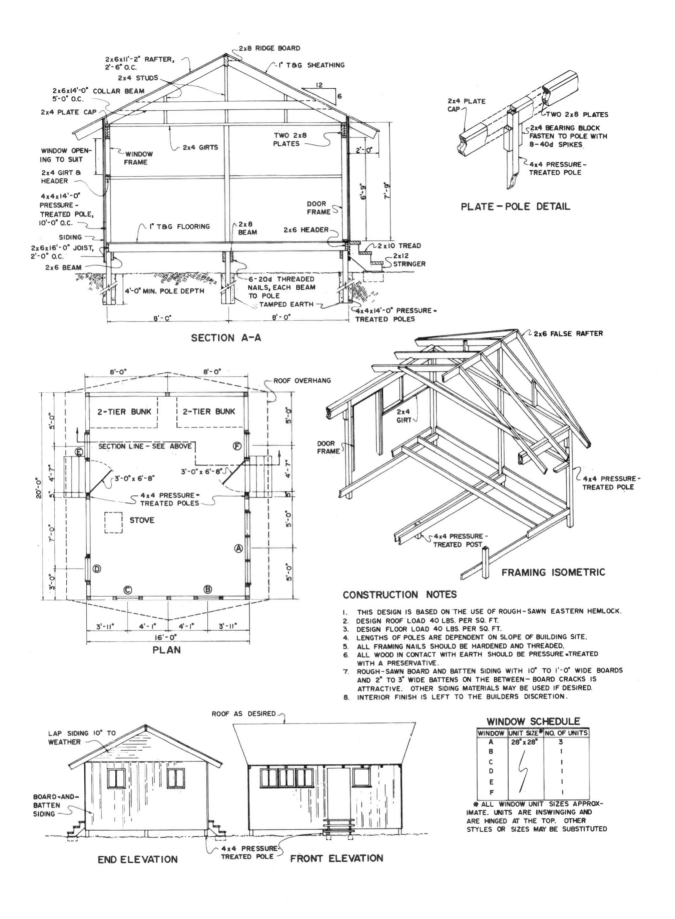

## SECTION A-A

2x8 RIDGE BOARD
1" T&G SHEATHING
2x6x11'-2" RAFTER, 2'-6" O.C.
2x4 STUDS
2x6x14'-0" COLLAR BEAM 5'-0" O.C.
2x4 PLATE CAP
WINDOW OPENING TO SUIT
WINDOW FRAME
2x4 GIRTS
TWO 2x8 PLATES
2x4 GIRT & HEADER
4x4x14'-0" PRESSURE-TREATED POLE, 10'-0" O.C.
DOOR FRAME
SIDING
1" T&G FLOORING
2x8 BEAM
2x6 HEADER
2x6x16'-0" JOIST, 2'-0" O.C.
2x6 BEAM
4'-0" MIN. POLE DEPTH
6-20d THREADED NAILS, EACH BEAM TO POLE
TAMPED EARTH
2x10 TREAD
2x12 STRINGER
4x4x14'-0" PRESSURE-TREATED POLES
8'-0"    8'-0"

## PLATE-POLE DETAIL

2x4 PLATE CAP
TWO 2x8 PLATES
2x4 BEARING BLOCK FASTEN TO POLE WITH 8-40d SPIKES
4x4 PRESSURE-TREATED POLE

## PLAN

8'-0"    8'-0"
ROOF OVERHANG
2-TIER BUNK    2-TIER BUNK
SECTION LINE - SEE ABOVE
3'-0" x 6'-8"
3'-0" x 6'-8"
4x4 PRESSURE-TREATED POLES
STOVE
5'-0"  4'-7"  5"  7'-0"  3'-0"
20'-0"
5'-0"  4'-7"  5'-0"  5'-0"
3'-11"  4'-1"  4'-1"  3'-11"
16'-0"

## FRAMING ISOMETRIC

2x6 FALSE RAFTER
2x4 GIRT
DOOR FRAME
4x4 PRESSURE-TREATED POLE
4x4 PRESSURE-TREATED POST

## CONSTRUCTION NOTES

1. THIS DESIGN IS BASED ON THE USE OF ROUGH-SAWN EASTERN HEMLOCK.
2. DESIGN ROOF LOAD 40 LBS. PER SQ. FT.
3. DESIGN FLOOR LOAD 40 LBS. PER SQ. FT.
4. LENGTHS OF POLES ARE DEPENDENT ON SLOPE OF BUILDING SITE.
5. ALL FRAMING NAILS SHOULD BE HARDENED AND THREADED.
6. ALL WOOD IN CONTACT WITH EARTH SHOULD BE PRESSURE-TREATED WITH A PRESERVATIVE.
7. ROUGH-SAWN BOARD AND BATTEN SIDING WITH 10" TO 1'-0" WIDE BOARDS AND 2" TO 3" WIDE BATTENS ON THE BETWEEN-BOARD CRACKS IS ATTRACTIVE. OTHER SIDING MATERIALS MAY BE USED IF DESIRED.
8. INTERIOR FINISH IS LEFT TO THE BUILDERS DISCRETION.

## WINDOW SCHEDULE

| WINDOW | UNIT SIZE* | NO. OF UNITS |
|--------|-----------|--------------|
| A | 28" x 28" | 3 |
| B | | 1 |
| C | | 1 |
| D | | 1 |
| E | | 1 |
| F | | 1 |

* ALL WINDOW UNIT SIZES APPROXIMATE. UNITS ARE INSWINGING AND ARE HINGED AT THE TOP. OTHER STYLES OR SIZES MAY BE SUBSTITUTED

## END ELEVATION

LAP SIDING 10" TO WEATHER
ROOF AS DESIRED
BOARD-AND-BATTEN SIDING

## FRONT ELEVATION

4x4 PRESSURE-TREATED POLE

# VACATION HOUSE, FRAME CONSTRUCTION, PLAN NO. 5997

Comfort, convenience, safety, and economy were designed into this house by agricultural engineers at Beltsville, Md. The heating system uniformly distributes heat from any type of heater—wood, coal, gas, or oil-fired. The standards of convenience and sanitation that are found in the most expensive home are maintained in this low-cost house. The framing timber is used efficiently so that cost of material is reduced without the loss of the framing strength. Wall panels, trusses, and floor systems were load-tested to prove the strength. This method of construction, described in Miscellaneous Publication 1020,[1] is recommended because it is low cost, and the simplified building techniques allow the home owner to do some of the work himself.

The outstanding features of this house are the post-and-girt construction and a free-floating floor that promotes central heating without ductwork—that is, perimeter distribution of warmed air. Besides these improvements in construction methods, the house plan embodies the usual cost-saving features—multiple use of space, minimum traffic lanes, and omission of unnecessary trim or doors.

[1] Newman, J.O. *A House-Framing System for Low-Cost Construction.* U.S. Dept. Agr. Misc. Pub. No. 1020, 18 pp. 1966.

SCALE IN FEET

## Post-and-girt construction

Pressure treated 4- by 6-inch posts, set 8 feet 4 inches on center, serve as foundation members; as the columnar support for the airtight, insulated, skirt wall around the crawl space; and as the columnar supports for the curtain-wall sides and roof. The built-up plate and lintel system is continuous around the entire periphery of the

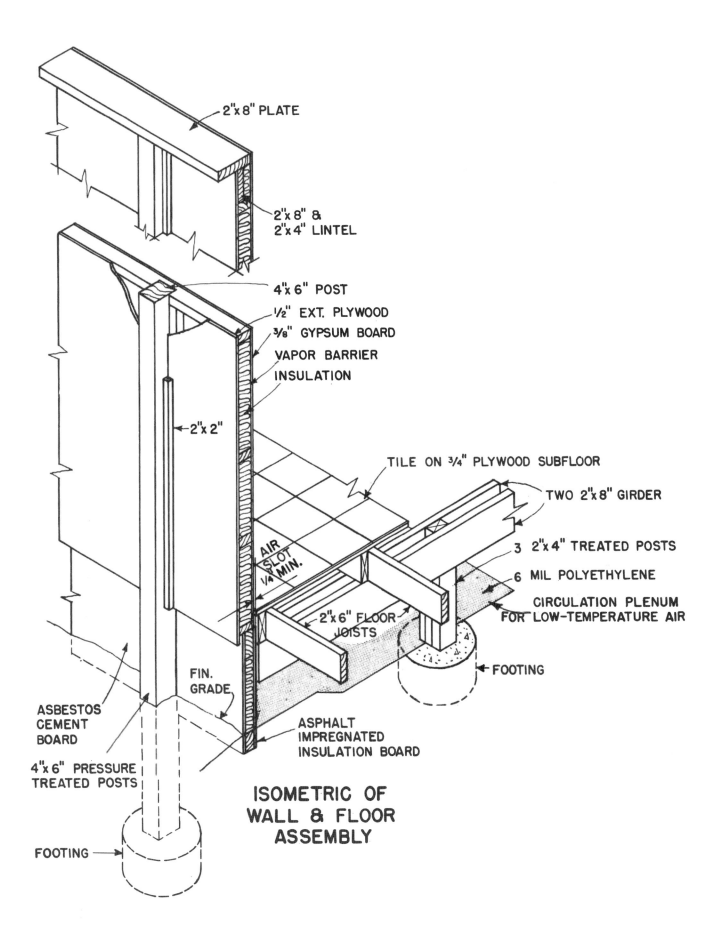

2"x 8" PLATE

2"x 8" &
2"x 4" LINTEL

4"x 6" POST
½" EXT. PLYWOOD
⅜" GYPSUM BOARD
VAPOR BARRIER
INSULATION

2"x 2"

TILE ON ¾" PLYWOOD SUBFLOOR

TWO 2"x 8" GIRDER

3 2"x 4" TREATED POSTS

6 MIL POLYETHYLENE

CIRCULATION PLENUM
FOR LOW-TEMPERATURE AIR

AIR
SLOT
¼ MIN.

2"x 6" FLOOR
JOISTS

FOOTING

FIN.
GRADE

ASBESTOS
CEMENT
BOARD

ASPHALT
IMPREGNATED
INSULATION BOARD

4"x 6" PRESSURE
TREATED POSTS

ISOMETRIC OF
WALL & FLOOR
ASSEMBLY

FOOTING

25

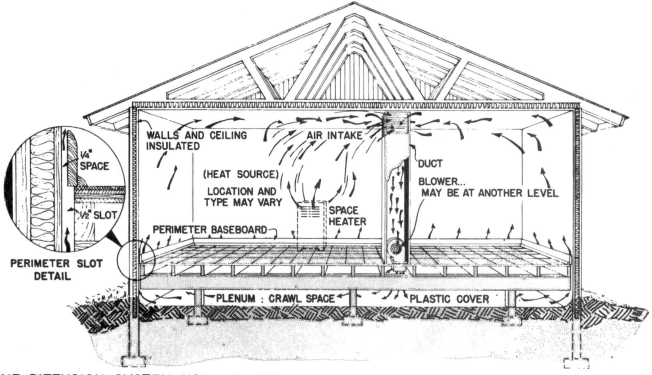

**AIR DIFFUSION SYSTEM USING UNDER-FLOOR PLENUM WITH PERIMETER SLOT**

house. No further lintels are needed over the doors and windows. The full 8-inch wide top plate member and the 8-inch deep lintel form an excellent foundation for fastening the roof trusses. A building with this continuous tie from the foundation through the trusses is more resistant to wind damage than a building with conventional platform framing.

Horizontal nail ties, 2 feet on center, are notched onto the posts for precision spacing and alinement—a help in speedy erection. The curtain wall sides are continuous on the interior, but are placed between the posts on the exterior. The skirt wall beneath the floor is a little over 2 inches thick and is installed on the inside of the posts. Because of its continuity, the skirt can easily be made airtight. No ventilators are installed in the crawl space of this house.

Continuous cantilevered joists and girders support the floor and carry the interior loads independently of the exterior loads and shrinkage. This improvement in construction technique prevents doors and windows from being pulled out of line and sticking. In conventional construction, floor settlement creates problems in the walls. With post-and-girt construction, the floor can be installed after the roof and walls are placed, and interior partitions can be installed after the floor and ceiling are in place.

## Superior heating at low cost

The perimeter-slot heating system used in this house provides draft-free comfort and a uniform temperature. A fan draws warm air from a centrally located intake near the ceiling and delivers it into the crawl space beneath the floor. Since air pressure in the crawl space is a little higher than that inside the house, air flows through the ¼-inch-wide slot around the entire periphery of the house. This air warms the floor and walls, and the result is draft-free uniform temperatures in the house.

The best uniformity of temperature distribution is maintained with continuous operation of the circulating fan. Temperature uniformity was somewhat better when the air was heated with a down-draft type of hot air furance than when it was heated with a space heater in one corner of the living room. However, tests of the heating systems show that while both of the above systems were superior to the perimeter loop type, the perimeter-slot heating system gave the best heat distribution at lower cost than the other systems.

26

# TENANT HOUSE, PLAN NO. 7010

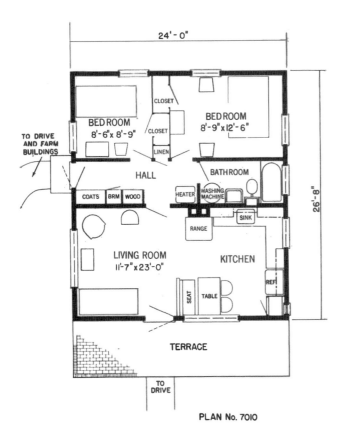

PLAN No. 7010

This minimum house is suitable for use as a tenant house or for the first home of a young married couple.

For economy and good use of space, the living room, dining room, and kitchen are combined into one large room. Folding screens may be used to separate the kitchen area from the main living room if desired.

A ventilated storage cabinet for food is provided, next to the refrigerator.

A double-deck bed could be used in the smaller of the two bedrooms. A deep, roll-rim sink in the bathroom serves as washbowl and laundry tray. There is space in the bathroom for a washing machine. In such a small house, the bathroom is a better place for doing the laundry than the cooking and living quarters.

A circulator heater or floor furnace can be installed in the back hall. The hall also contains work clothes and general utility closets.

The pipes for all plumbing fixtures are in one partition—which means that they can be installed with the greatest economy.

With the gable roof, the house can be expanded or the interior rearranged later at minimum expense. The roof is trussed, so there are no interior bearing partitions.

With the flat roof, the center partition of the house is a bearing partition, but other partitions can easily be moved. This style is usually a little cheaper to build than the gabled style.

27

# FARM COTTAGE, PLAN NO. 7137

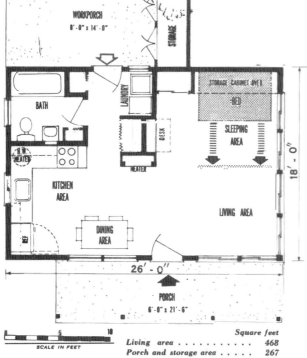

Square feet
Living area . . . . . . . . . . . . 468
Porch and storage area . . . . . 267

This small frame cottage represents a practical minimum of both space and cost. It is intended primarily for a young couple starting out on a farm. Later, when the farm business is further developed, it can be used as a tenant house.

The cottage is also adequate for a retired couple who do not wish to maintain a large house.

Special space-saving features include an under-the-counter water heater, a pullout bed, a wall-type heater with a prefabricated metal or asbestos-cement chimney, a wall desk, and accordion-type closet doors.

With large porches and generous window areas, the cottage is particularly suitable for warm climates.

## Interior

The view of the sleeping area shows the convertible bed in the pulled-out position. The bed becomes a comfortable couch for daytime use when pushed partly under the storage cabinet and provided with cushions for a back rest.

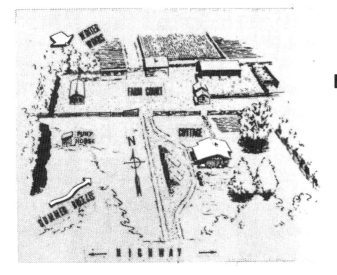

## Farmstead layout

The cottage should be located at least 100 feet from the highway and about the same distance from the farm court, to keep out odors and dust from the livestock area.

If a second dwelling is built, it may be located at the left of this arrangement, with a separate driveway from the highway.

# ADIRONDACK-TYPE SHELTER, PLAN NO. 5998

The Adirondack-type shelter fills the recreational needs for scout camps, hunting shelters, and overnight accommodations on the foot trail. It also may be used on a suburban lot as a playhouse or storage place for garden tools and recreational equipment. Some shelters have been used as market stands for fresh farm produce. In Massachusetts, where the shelter was developed, it has many uses and is in popular demand.

The pole-type construction, designed to fit the skill of beginning carpenters, is economical and easy to erect. When properly treated with preservatives, the poles will last from 30 to 75 years.

The rafters are trussed units, prefabricated on the ground in a jig for bolt location. The roof is designed to carry a load of 30 pounds per square foot.

The builder has a wide choice of materials for the floor, sidewalls, and roof. The floor can be of concrete, but tamped earth or gravel may be substituted. Sidewalls are rough-sawn, 1- by 10-inch eastern hemlock boards that are battened with 2- to 3-inch strips; the tongue-and-groove roof can be covered with a waterproofing surface, such as cedar or asphalt shingles, composition roll roofing, steel, aluminum, or terne.

A carefully selected building site can mean the difference between success and failure of the shelter. The back of the shelter should face the wind, and the front should slope forward to keep storm water off the floor. If the shelter is to be used in winter, it should be protected from direct winds to keep snow from drifting in the front. An open-front shelter should face south. The front can be closed in for protection against weather and for storage.

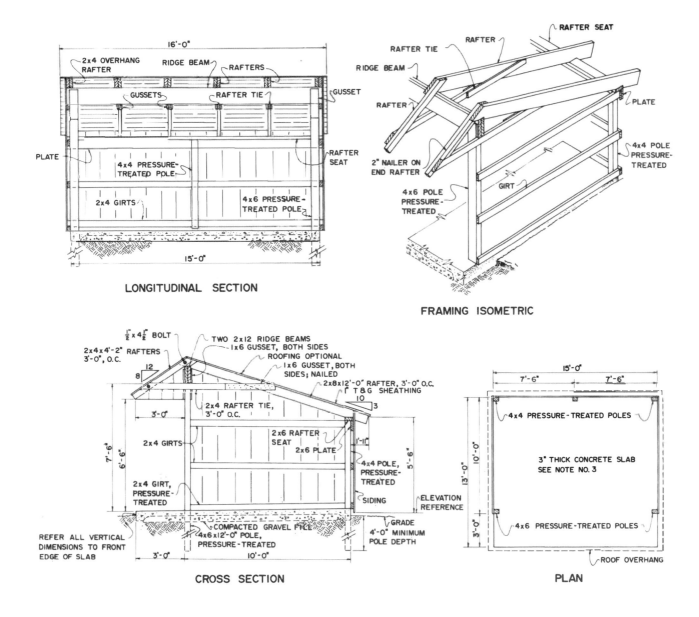

LONGITUDINAL SECTION

FRAMING ISOMETRIC

CROSS SECTION

PLAN

1. PREPARE CONCRETE FLOOR SLAB WITH THICKENED EDGE, 9 INCHES DEEP BY 6 INCHES WIDE, ALONG THE BOTTOM SURFACE.

2. SLOPE FLOOR 1/4 INCH PER FOOT FROM REAR TO FRONT AND INCREASE ALONG THE 3-FOOT FRONT APRON TO MINIMIZE PUDDLING FROM WIND-DRIVEN RAIN.

3. USE CONCRETE MIX WITH 3/4-INCH MAXIMUM SIZE AGGREGATE; 6 1/2 SACKS CEMENT PER CUBIC YARD, 6 GALLONS WATER PER SACK OF CEMENT (1 SACK EQUALS 1 CUBIC FOOT), AND 6 PERCENT ENTRAINED AIR BY VOLUME.

4. ERECT THE 4- BY 6-INCH POLES WITH RIDGE BEAM FIRST; THEN LOCATE THE REAR WALL POLES.

5. DETACH THE SHORT 2- BY 4-INCH RAFTER OVERHANG FROM UNIT; POSITION 2- BY 8-INCH PRIMARY RAFTER AND TIE RAFTER ON OUTSIDE OF OVERHANG AT BOTH ENDS OF BUILDING.

6. THEN BOLT OVERHANG IN PLACE.

491-229 O - 73 - 5

# BARNS AND EQUIPMENT FOR HORSES

## EXPANSIBLE BARN FOR RIDING HORSES, PLAN NO. 5838

This small barn was designed for use in hot, moderate, or cold climates. In very cold or hot climates, the low-pitched roof should be insulated.

The construction is frame. Floors in the feed and tack rooms are concrete; stall floors are clay. The two 12- by 12-foot box stalls are separated by a plank partition open at the top. Built-up roofing surfaced with white stone chips (mineral granules) to reflect heat is suggested.

Length of the building may be increased as desired to provide additional stalls or feed storage.

The structure is designed to withstand snow loads up to 20 pounds per square foot or winds that do not exceed 75 m.p.h. If the girder size and rafter spacing are changed as noted on the working plans, the barn is suitable for use in areas subject to 30-pound snow loads or winds of hurricane force.

Working plans show an alternate, more steeply pitched roof. This is for use where the appearance of the building must conform to that of adjacent buildings or where additional mow space for hay and bedding storage is desired. If he selects the alternate plan, the owner may prefer to use the tack room as a feed room and the present feed room as a combination tack and bunk room.

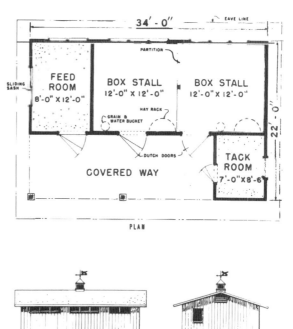

PLAN

REAR ELEVATION          RIGHT END ELEVATION

32

# TWO-HORSE TRAILER, PLAN NO. 5943

Skilled mechanics with good metal-cutting and welding equipment can construct this four-wheel, tandem-axle, two-horse trailer. It is not a job for the average do-it-yourselfer. Commercial drop axles can be substituted for the axles shown and other changes can be made to suit the parts and materials that are available.

Stability of the vehicle, the primary concern in transporting horses, is achieved with the use of tandem axles, a padded chest bar, and a dividing bar that is secured with a padded tail chain. The dividing bar can be removed so the trailer can be used for hauling wider loads. Saddles and gear are carried in the space in front of the chest bar; and when the trailer is parked, it can be used for feeding and watering the animals.

A narrow door at the front of the trailer permits a person to exit from that end after he leads a horse into the van. The inclined back gate serves as a loading ramp. This 2-ton-capacity trailer is a valuable working tool for the rancher because it is easy to load.

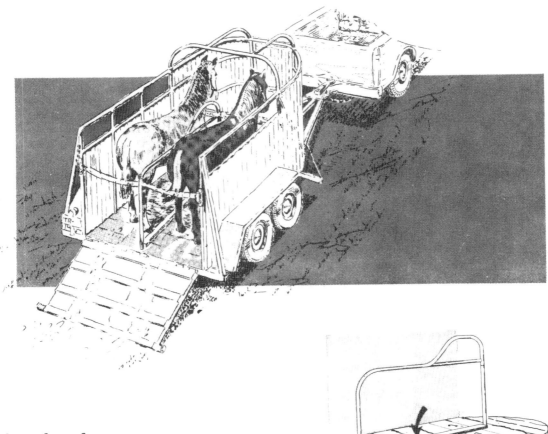

## Built-in safety features

The same precautions used in constructing any trailer must be strictly followed in constructing a horse trailer. It must be equipped with brakes, brake light, taillight, and a safety chain on the hitch. Both electric and hydraulic brakes are available for trailers. The tailgate pins should be drilled for safety rings or pins.

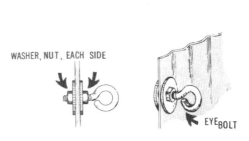

WASHER, NUT, EACH SIDE

EYE BOLT

## Tandem axles have advantages and disadvantages

The advantages of tandem axles outweigh the disadvantages. Tandem-axle trailers are safer, have less sway, and put smaller loads on the towing vehicle than do single axle trailers.

A disadvantage of the tandem axle is that the hitch is seldom at the proper height for maximum stability of the trailer. To build the hitch height as nearly right as possible, the towing vehicle should be set on a level site. As shown in the schematic sketch, when the towing point is too high, the front tires of the trailer tend to leave the ground; and when the towing point is too low, the rear tires of the trailer tend to leave the ground.

Proper hitch height is more important for a trailer without springs than it is for a trailer with spring action that permits the axles to ride at different heights.

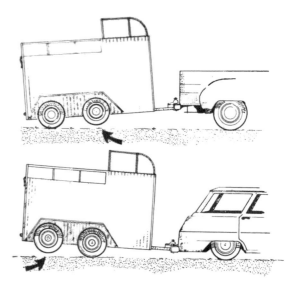

## Antirattle construction

This trailer is prone to rattle unless precautions are taken in fastening it together. Neoprene washers should be inserted between the covering and the frame whenever a self-tapping screw is used to fasten the cover. Corrugated gasket strips installed between covering metal and frame helps prevent rattles. Also, some covering materials are inherently less noisy than sheet steel.

Horses that are being transported should be carefully protected from injury. For instance, the chest bar must be padded to prevent localized injury or galling. Burlap sacking, wrapped and tied around the bar, makes good padding. A rough and uneven floor surface keeps the horses' feet from sliding. A floor of rough-sawn oak boards, which usually vary in thickness, provides the desirable uneven surface. A smooth floor should be covered with heavy matting material that will not become slick. Matting with interwoven wire should be

avoided. A 2 by 4 fastened beneath the center divider, as shown in the illustration, will prevent the horses from slipping sideways.

Protection is also needed to keep the horses free from drafts, especially when the animals are hot and sweaty. The front wall of the trailer will provide this protection if it is high enough to cut direct wind from the animals. Seventy-two inches is high enough for quarter horses, but thoroughbreds and hunters may require a wall height of as much as 85 inches. A well-fitted canvas cover for the canopy frame will also provide protection. Ordinary double-nutted eyebolts (see illustration) with large washers can be installed in the trailer front and will serve to hold the lashing for the cover.

Other safety features used will depend somewhat on the horses being carried. Nervous or frightened animals may need a solid, center divider between them. Sometimes the sides of the van and the divider bars are padded to prevent bruising or abrasion of the horses.

# SADDLE HORSE BARN, PLAN NO. 5994

This barn for saddle horses is easy to build, pleasing in appearance, and designed for long life and low-cost maintenance because it is a well-anchored, pole-type construction. Treated posts are set in concrete, the girder is steel-strapped to posts, and rafters are anchored to girder and are lapped and bolted at the ridge. Strong construction at these four places makes a wind-resistive building. After the 2-inch kickboards are placed to aline the building, concrete should be used to backfill around the posts.

The recommended dimensions of the barn minimize waste of construction material.

Translucent panels in the front wall admit a pleasing amount of diffused light into the stable. The upper half of the weather protected dutch doors at stall entrances can be opened in mild weather to provide cross ventilation from the rear window. These doors provide air movement in the upper part of the stalls and draft-free ventilation in summer and winter.

Some details of construction for various parts of the building are shown on the illustration.

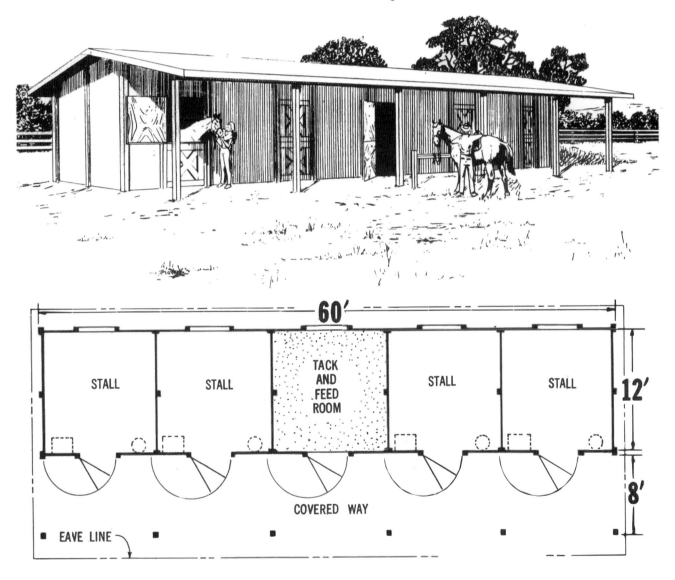

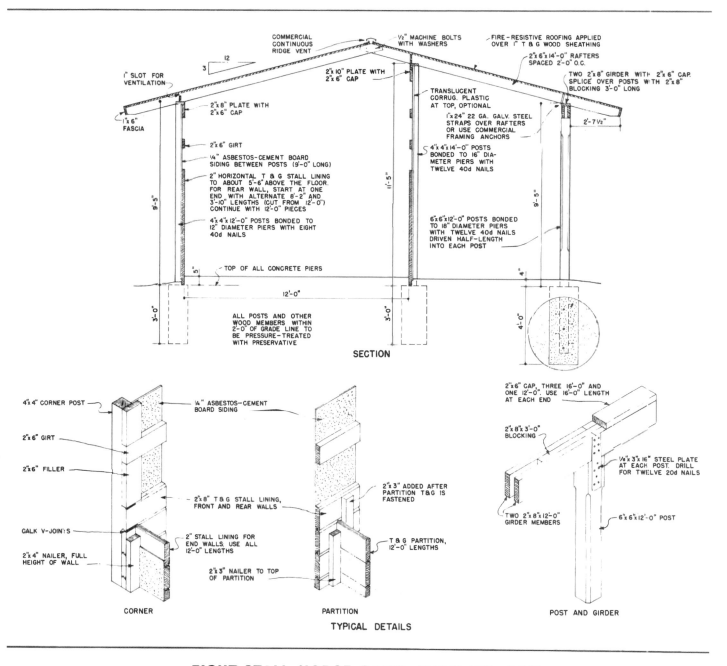

**SECTION**

**TYPICAL DETAILS**

CORNER

PARTITION

POST AND GIRDER

# EIGHT-STALL HORSE BARN, PLAN NO. 6010

Convenience, economy of space, durability and economy of materials, good drainage, lighting, ventilation, and warmth should all be considered in planning horse barns.

This barn, designed by the Virginia Polytechnic Institute (VPI) is for use by farmers who wish to establish recreational facilities on their property for added income. The plan was submitted by the VPI to the Southern Plan Exchange for national distribution by the Cooperative Farm Building Plan Exchange.

The building is 24 feet wide by 50 feet long and contains eight stalls, a feed room, and a tack room. Its length is variable in units of 10 feet.

Planned for economy, long life, and low-cost maintenance, the barn is of pole- or post-type construction and is easy to build. All the poles or posts, splashboards, and other wood parts that will come in contact with the ground or with manure should be pressure treated with preservative to a retention of 8 pounds per cubic foot.

Feed room and tack room floors are of concrete and stall floors are of tamped clay.

The wood roof trusses are securely fastened to the girder and plate with 22-gage galvanized steel straps or with commercial type framing anchors. Two-and one-half-inch corrugated metal is suggested for the roof

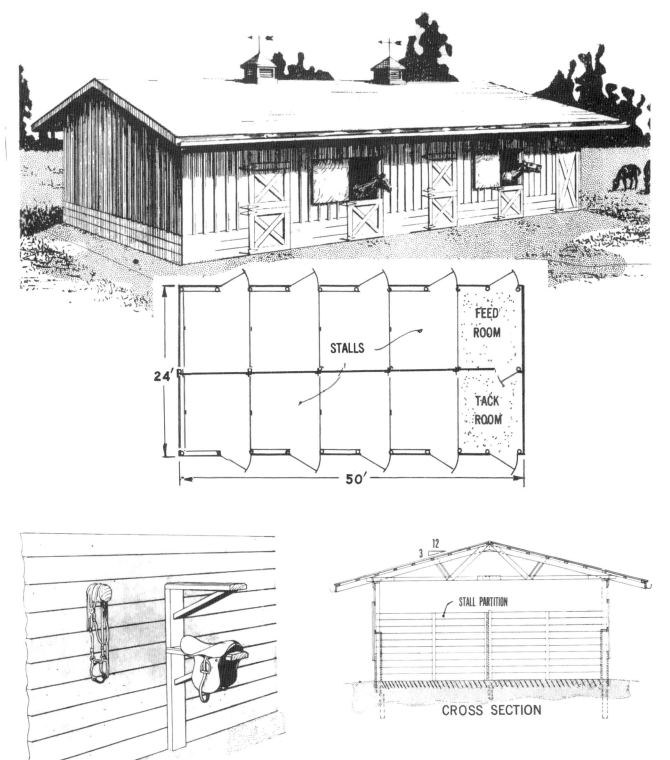

FEED ROOM

STALLS

TACK ROOM

24'

50'

SADDLE RACK

3 12

STALL PARTITION

CROSS SECTION

covering. A 4-foot overhang, built into the roof design, provides partial shelter along the building sides.

The box stalls, approximately 10 by 12 feet, are constructed of 2-inch lumber. The dutch doors on the exterior walls of the stalls open outward to a paddock or pasture. The lower 2 feet of the stall walls should be treated with a preservative that is noninjurious to the animals.

Wood or metal siding is suitable for the exterior walls. If metal siding is used, it is essential that a kicker panel of 2-inch lumber be constructed on the interior surface of the exterior framing.

The two cupolas shown on the working drawings can be purchased preconstructed from a lumber and millwork dealer. The bridle and saddle racks shown on the drawings are easily constructed.

The saddle racks in the tack room should be spaced 24 to 30 inches apart. The lower and upper racks should be 36 inches and 60 inches, respectively, above the floor.

# SEVENTEEN-STALL HORSE BARN, PLAN NO. 6011

Horseback riding has become popular throughout most of the United States. Numerous private and public riding clubs and academies are available to those who enjoy the sport of horsemanship. Some State and National parks also offer riding horses for hire. The farmer who wishes to supplement his income may establish such a recreational facility on his property.

This barn plan, designed by the Virginia Polytechnic Institute, is for the farmer who is interested in operating a horseback riding facility as a money-making sideline. The barn is designed for economy, long life, and low-cost maintenance. It is of pole-type construction and is easy to build. The dimensions are 36 by 100 feet, and the length of the building is variable in 10-foot units. All poles, splashboards, and other wood parts that come in contact with the ground or manure should be pressure-treated with preservative to a retention of 8 pounds per cubic foot.

A center alley separates the two rows of stalls and is wide enough for the chore of saddling horses. A tack room and a feed room are located in the back end of the building. Above the center alley is a hay mow or storage loft. Hay can be dropped from the loft directly into the stalls, thereby eliminating some of the traffic between the feed room and the stalls.

Floors are concrete in the feed room and in the tack room, clay in the stalls and in the center alley, and wood in the loft. The loft floor is designed to withstand a load not to exceed 75 pounds per square foot.

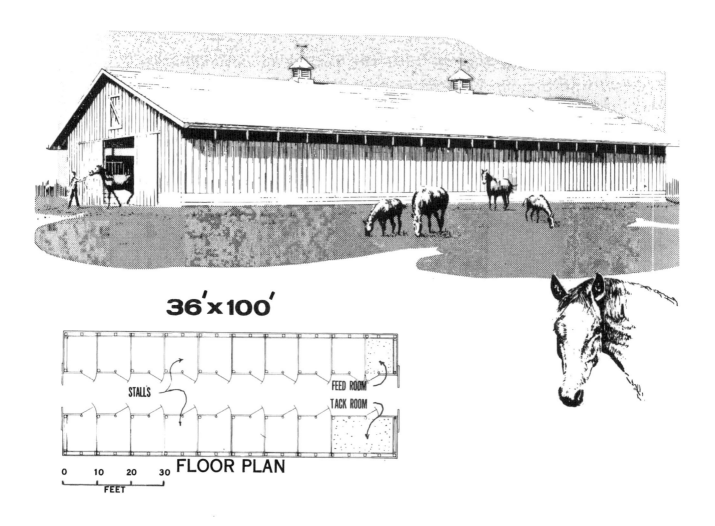

**36'x100'**

STALLS

FEED ROOM

TACK ROOM

**FLOOR PLAN**

0  10  20  30

FEET

The wood roof framing is securely fastened to wood beams with 22-gage steel straps or with commercial framing anchors. A covering of 2½-inch corrugated metal is suggested for the roof exterior.

The 10- by 12-foot box stalls are constructed with 2-inch lumber. For the protection of the animals, the lower 2 feet of the walls should be treated with a nontoxic preservative. The working plans show alternate stall details and an alternate roof design using trusses.

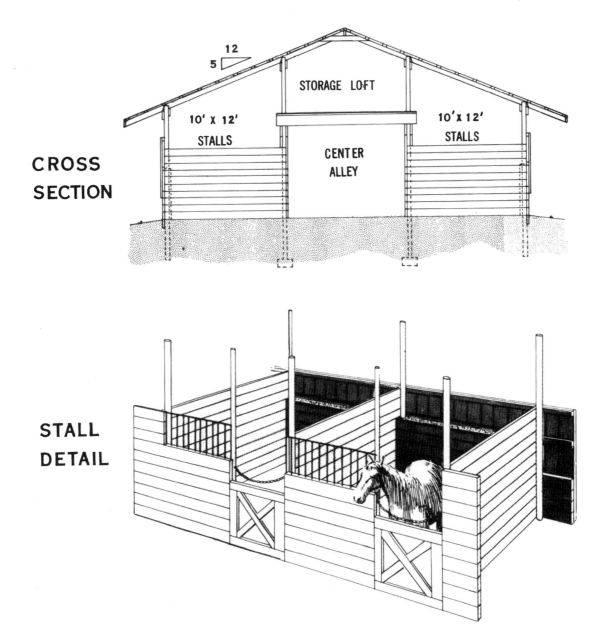

CROSS SECTION

STALL DETAIL

# ONE-AND-A-HALF-STORY HORSE BARN, PLAN NO. 6024

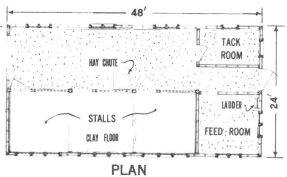

PLAN

Labor saving devices developed by science and technology have made it possible for farm families to use their leisure time to increase their income by establishing recreational facilities on their farm property. One such facility may be a riding academy.

This 1½-story, gambrel-roofed barn for horses is well suited to many farmsteads and has a pleasingly traditional appearance. It was designed at Rutgers University, New Brunswick, N.J., and was submitted to the Northeast Plan Exchange for national distribution through the Cooperative Farm Building Plan Exchange.

The barn is particularly well suited for use in the colder parts of the United States. The alleyway along the front of the stall row and the hay and bedding storage space overhead are enclosed. The feed and tack rooms are on the ground level.

Floors of tamped clay in the stalls and of concrete in the other first floor areas are recommended.

The building, 24 feet wide by 48 feet long, contains three 12- by 12-foot stalls and a 12- by 36-foot working alley, convenient for grooming the horses and for doing other chores. The concrete foundation walls are 1 foot above ground level and, with the concrete footings, they extend below the frostline.

The building is frame construction throughout with 2- by 4-inch studs 2 feet on centers and with fire-stopping materials midway between the sill and the upper plate.

Although the exterior walls indicate the use of horizontal siding, larger sheet materials, such as exterior plywood, may be used. The interior walls of the stalls are covered with 2-inch planking up to the firestop level, and all interior surfaces of the exterior walls are covered with 1-inch sheathing.

The stable ceiling is covered with plywood, a vapor barrier, and insulating material.

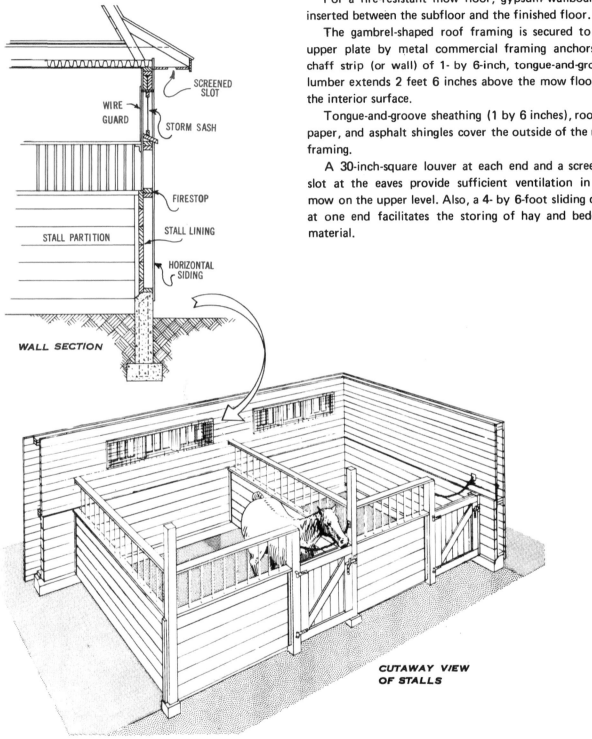

For a fire-resistant mow floor, gypsum wallboard is inserted between the subfloor and the finished floor.

The gambrel-shaped roof framing is secured to the upper plate by metal commercial framing anchors. A chaff strip (or wall) of 1- by 6-inch, tongue-and-groove lumber extends 2 feet 6 inches above the mow floor on the interior surface.

Tongue-and-groove sheathing (1 by 6 inches), roofing paper, and asphalt shingles cover the outside of the roof framing.

A 30-inch-square louver at each end and a screened slot at the eaves provide sufficient ventilation in the mow on the upper level. Also, a 4- by 6-foot sliding door at one end facilitates the storing of hay and bedding material.

SCREENED SLOT

WIRE GUARD

STORM SASH

FIRESTOP

STALL LINING

STALL PARTITION

HORIZONTAL SIDING

WALL SECTION

CUTAWAY VIEW OF STALLS

# PORTABLE STABLE FOR A HORSE, PLAN NO. 6082

This portable, one-horse stable was designed at Rutgers University, New Brunswick, N.J., with emphasis on the economical use of materials.

The openings between the rafters at front and rear of the building, two hinged panels that open in the rear wall, and a dutch door provide ventilation. The windows in the sidewalls are optional.

The plan for the stable does not show a floor covering. However, well-tamped clay makes a very good floor for a horse stable and is preferable to a wood floor. The clay should be built up enough so that the floor will be several inches above the outside ground level. The walls can then be tilted up and secured to the pressure-treated timber base. The exterior-type plywood siding stiffens the walls, eliminating the need for let-in braces. The roofing is corrugated metal and translucent plastic.

No interior wall lining is shown on the working drawings but may be desirable, depending on the temperament of the horse and the preference of the horseman.

In areas subject to high winds, the stable should be securely anchored in place.

**CAUTION:** Do not use paint containing lead on any part of buildings, fences, or equipment that is accessible to livestock.

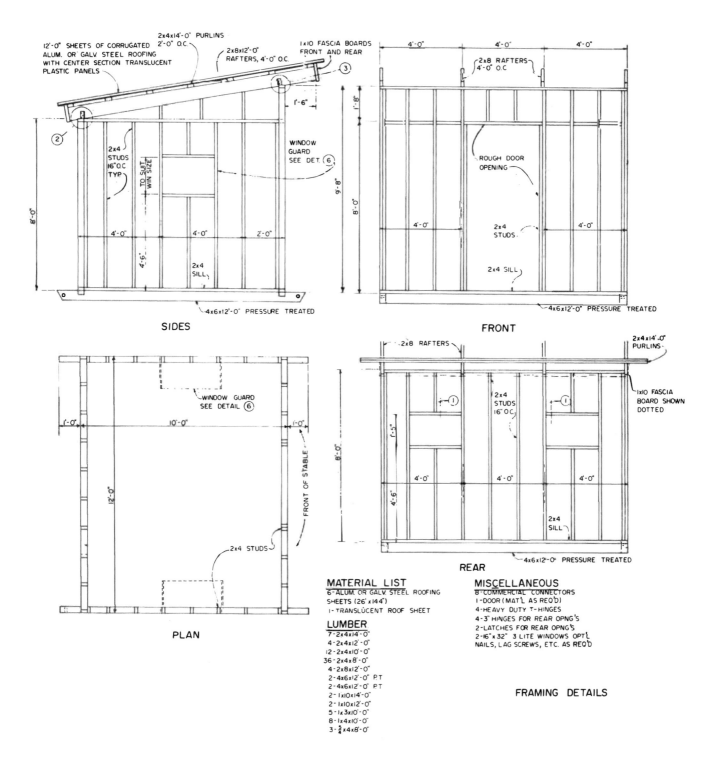

12'-0" SHEETS OF CORRUGATED ALUM. OR GALV STEEL ROOFING WITH CENTER SECTION TRANSLUCENT PLASTIC PANELS

2x4x14'-0" PURLINS 2'-0" O.C.

2x8x12'-0" RAFTERS, 4'-0" O.C.

1x10 FASCIA BOARDS FRONT AND REAR

③

①

1'-6"

②

2x4 STUDS 16" O.C TYP

TO SUIT WIN SIZE

WINDOW GUARD SEE DET. ⑥

8'-0"

4'-0"

4'-0"

2'-0"

4'-6"

2x4 SILL

4x6x12'-0" PRESSURE TREATED

SIDES

4'-0"    4'-0"    4'-0"

2x8 RAFTERS 4'-0" O.C.

1'-8"

ROUGH DOOR OPENING

9'-8"

8'-0"

4'-0"

2x4 STUDS

4'-0"

2x4 SILL

4x6x12'-0" PRESSURE TREATED

FRONT

1'-0"

10'-0"

1'-0"

WINDOW GUARD SEE DETAIL ⑥

12'-0"

FRONT OF STABLE

2x4 STUDS

PLAN

2x8 RAFTERS

2x4x14'-0" PURLINS

1x10 FASCIA BOARD SHOWN DOTTED

①    ①

2x4 STUDS 16" O.C.

1'-5"

8'-0"

4'-0"    4'-0"    4'-0"

4'-6"

2x4 SILL

4x6x12'-0" PRESSURE TREATED

REAR

## MATERIAL LIST
6- ALUM. OR GALV. STEEL ROOFING SHEETS (26"x144")
1- TRANSLUCENT ROOF SHEET

### LUMBER
7 - 2x4x14'-0"
4 - 2x4x12'-0"
12 - 2x4x10'-0"
36 - 2x4x8'-0"
4 - 2x8x12'-0"
2 - 4x6x12'-0" P.T
2 - 4x6x12'-0" P.T
2 - 1x10x14'-0"
2 - 1x10x12'-0"
5 - 1x3x10'-0"
8 - 1x4x10'-0"
3 - ¾x4x8'-0"

## MISCELLANEOUS
8- COMMERCIAL CONNECTORS
1- DOOR (MAT'L AS REQ'D)
4- HEAVY DUTY T-HINGES
4- 3" HINGES FOR REAR OPNG'S
2- LATCHES FOR REAR OPNG'S
2- 16"x 32" 3 LITE WINDOWS OPT'L
NAILS, LAG SCREWS, ETC. AS REQ'D

FRAMING DETAILS

# HORSE EQUIPMENT, PLAN NO. 6014

The growing interest in the production and training of horses for field events—in the show ring and for hunting—is providing a profitable side line for many farmers.

The horse that will be used for cross-country hunting should be trained to jump so it will be able to clear the many obstacles it will encounter in the hunt. The same training can be used to good advantage for show horses.

The wood obstacles illustrated here are of the type used in training horses for show and for hunting.

The wood that will come in contact with the ground or that will be exposed to the weather should be treated with preservative for longer life of the equipment. A nonstaining preservative should be used so that the equipment can be painted. Rustproof fastenings are also recommended.

Construction details are shown in the four sheets of working drawings.

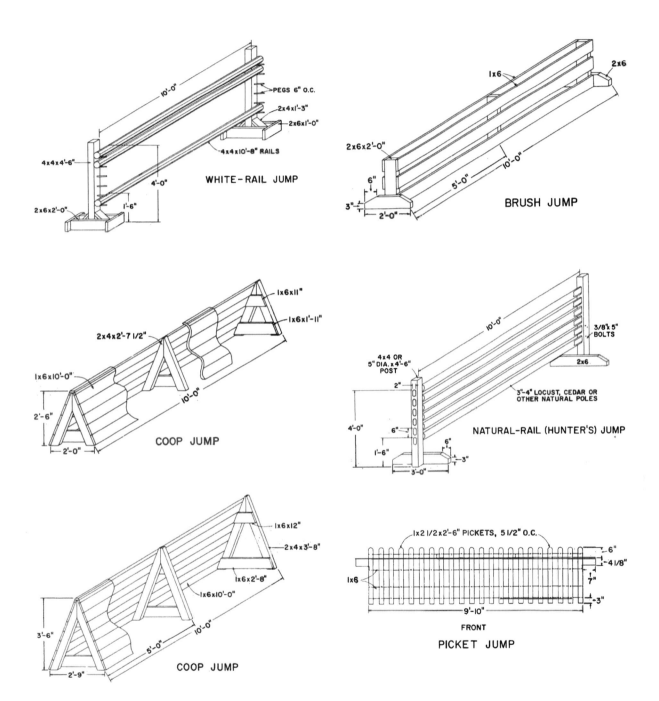

PEGS 6" O.C.

2x4x1'-3"

2x6x1'-0"

10'-0"

4x4x10'-8" RAILS

4x4x4'-6"

4'-0"

2x6x2'-0"

1'-6"

**WHITE-RAIL JUMP**

1x6

2x6

2x6x2'-0"

10'-0"

5'-0"

6"

3"

2'-0"

**BRUSH JUMP**

1x6x11"

1x6x1'-11"

2x4x2'-7 1/2"

1x6x10'-0"

10'-0"

2'-6"

2'-0"

**COOP JUMP**

10'-0"

4x4 OR
5" DIA. x 4'-6"
POST

2"

4'-0"

6"

1'-6"

6"

3"

3'-0"

3/8"x 5"
BOLTS

2x6

3"-4" LOCUST, CEDAR OR
OTHER NATURAL POLES

**NATURAL-RAIL (HUNTER'S) JUMP**

1x6x12"

2x4x3'-8"

1x6x2'-8"

1x6x10'-0"

3'-6"

10'-0"

5'-0"

2'-9"

**COOP JUMP**

1x2 1/2x2'-6" PICKETS, 5 1/2" O.C.

6"

4 1/8"

1x6

7"

3"

9'-10"

**FRONT**

**PICKET JUMP**

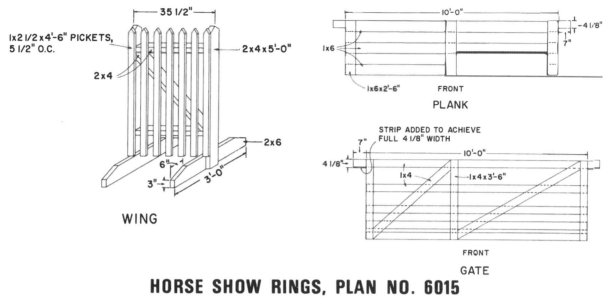

WING

PLANK

STRIP ADDED TO ACHIEVE
FULL 4 1/8" WIDTH

FRONT
GATE

# HORSE SHOW RINGS, PLAN NO. 6015

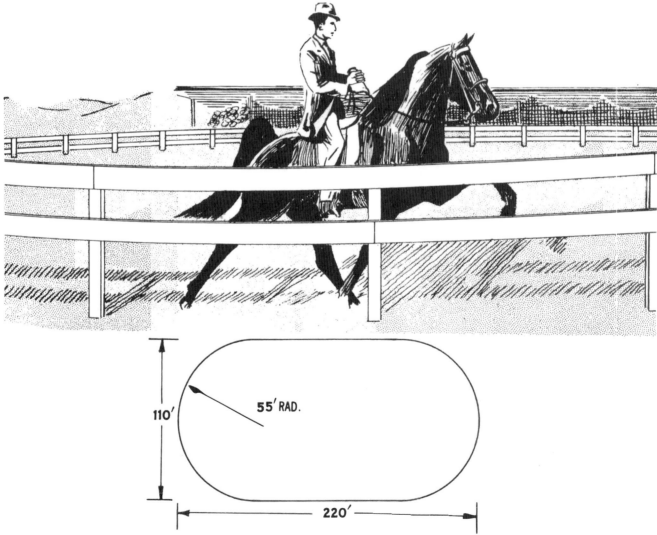

The plan for these indoor and outdoor show rings was developed at the Virginia Polytechnic Institute because of growing interest and demand for riding horses. Raising this type horse has now become a profitable business.

The show ring is considered an ideal place to exhibit horses for their performance, presence, quality, manners, all-around excellence, body conformation, and for gait—such as walk, trot, and canter. The use of the horse show ring benefits both the prospective buyer and the salesman.

The construction of the show rings is fairly simple. The boards, natural-rail, and movable fence should be treated with a nontoxic preservative for longer life of these parts. Noncorrosive fastenings should be used throughout the structures.

A section of movable fence, a gate, or removable rails can provide entrance to the ring. The ring sizes shown in the illustration were recommended by the National Horse Show Association, 307 West 49th Street, New York, N.Y. 10019.

The business of training horses for field events requires the use of special equipment such as that featured in Plan No. 6014, page 44. Construction details are shown in the plan for various types of jumps and related equipment.

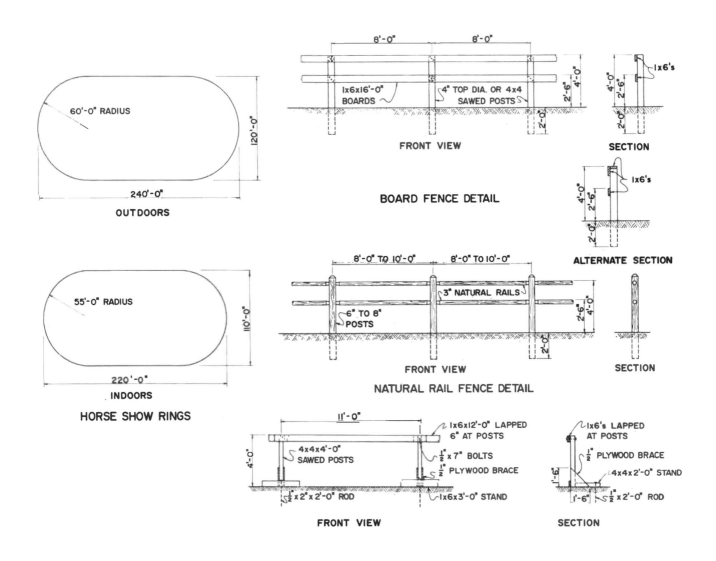

# GREENHOUSES

## PLASTIC-COVERED GREENHOUSE, PLAN NO. 5941

This plastic-covered greenhouse features a removable upper unit that can be used as a coldframe in which plants may be given a headstart on the frost-free season.

A heating cable can be installed in the assembled lower unit for germinating seeds and growing starter plants. When the plants are about 3 inches high, they should be moved to a coldframe located in a corner of the garden. The upper part of the greenhouse can then be placed over the plants to protect them from the night frost.

The wooden parts of the greenhouse frame should be pressure treated to prevent rotting. All hardware, including nails, should be galvanized.

The greenhouse should be anchored to the ground with steel rods.

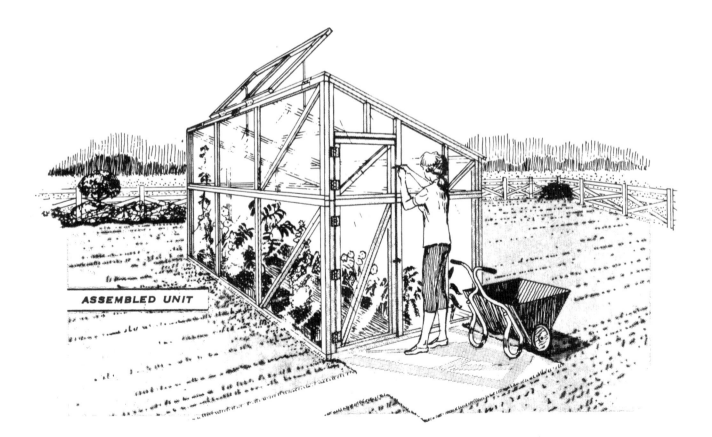

ASSEMBLED UNIT

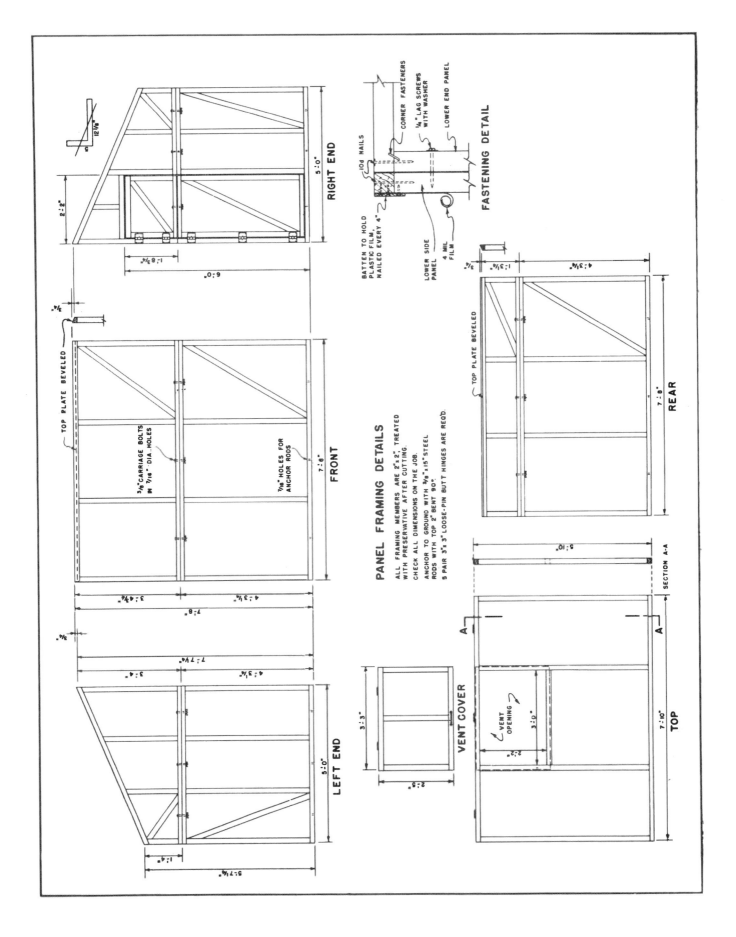

RIGHT END

12 ⅛"

2'-2"

5'-0"

1'-9 ¾"

9'-0"

CORNER FASTENERS

¼" LAG SCREWS WITH WASHER

LOWER END PANEL

10d NAILS

BATTEN TO HOLD PLASTIC FILM, NAILED EVERY 4"

LOWER SIDE PANEL

4 MIL FILM

**FASTENING DETAIL**

TOP PLATE BEVELED

¾"

FRONT

7'-8"

⅜"CARRIAGE BOLTS IN ⁷⁄₁₆" DIA. HOLES

⁷⁄₁₆" HOLES FOR ANCHOR RODS

3'-4 ¾"

7'-8"

7'-7 ¼"

3'-4"

4'-3 ⅛"

3'-4"

4'-3 ⅛"

¾"

**PANEL FRAMING DETAILS**

ALL FRAMING MEMBERS ARE 2"x2", TREATED WITH PRESERVATIVE AFTER CUTTING.
CHECK ALL DIMENSIONS ON THE JOB.
ANCHOR TO GROUND WITH ⅜"x15"STEEL RODS WITH TOP 2" BENT 90°.
5 PAIR 3"x 3" LOOSE-PIN BUTT HINGES ARE REQ'D.

TOP PLATE BEVELED

REAR

1'-3 ⅛"

4'-3 ⅛"

7'-8"

⅜"

LEFT END

5'-0"

1'-1"

5'-7 ¼"

VENT COVER

3'-3"

2'-8"

SECTION A-A

5'-10"

A

A

**TOP**

VENT OPENING

2'-2"

3'-0"

7'-10"

49

# PLASTIC-COVERED GREENHOUSE, PLAN NO. 5946

This greenhouse is easily constructed, inexpensive, and portable. Its roof slope approximates that of a gothic arch that extends from the ground to the ridge. The slope is steep enough to shed snow, water, and debris. However, a large accumulation of snow may pile up against the sides and cause lateral pressure to the plastic film.

The structure resists wind very well. A low-cost polyethylene cover will last from 3 to 8 months. More expensive films last from 2½ to 3 years or even longer. The film must be securely fastened to the frame, and the house must be staked down to resist strong winds.

In late summer, the plastic film can be replaced by a lath-type snow fence, and the house can be used as a propagating frame.

Two small ventilators at the top of the door provide limited ventilation. When more air is needed on hot days, the doors can be opened, or the house can be raised off the ground.

The width of the greenhouse (8½ feet) allows space for a walkway with a row of flats on each side, and the height (7 feet) allows head room for most people. With doors in each end, several units of this greenhouse can be placed in a series, and tools can be moved from section to section.

When the structure is finished, two men can move it short distances, and three or four men can lift it above their heads. It can also be placed on a flat-bed truck and moved to the desired location. Construction is rather simple, requiring only a little experience with common tools. The most complicated job—forming the ridge beam—is easy if a table saw with an adjustable table or blade is available to rip the board.

## Construction features

The base of the greenhouse is 12 feet long, 8 feet 6 inches wide, and 16 inches deep. Door frames are attached at each end and are tied together at the top with a beam which forms the center ridge of the greenhouse.

The ridge beam is constructed from a 1- by 10-inch board the length of the house. The board is ripped lengthwise near its center at an angle of 60° with the surface of the board. The two pieces are then fitted together to form a 120° angle. The relative position of these pieces is secured by fastening them together with wood screws spaced at 6-inch intervals.

The ridge board is supported on top of the door frames by a short 2 by 4 with a pointed end that fits into the beam's 120° angle. Plywood strips (¼ by 4 inches by 8 feet) that extend from the ridge board to the sides of the bottomless box form ribs along the sides. Each rib consists of two ¼-inch strips; they are bolted together at 1-foot intervals after they are in place. The sides and top of the house are covered with a single sheet of plastic 12 by 16 feet. Smaller sheets of plastic cover the ends and the doors. Batten strips are nailed to the ribs and over the edges of the plastic cover to hold it in place.

**A** *Ready for Assembling*

**B** *Taking Shape*

**C** *Securing Ridge Beam*

**D** *Fastening Plywood Bands*

**E** *Ready for Plastic Cover*

**F** *Moving to Location for Use*

51

# GREENHOUSE FRAMING FOR PLASTIC COVERING, PLAN NO. 6029

This building is of wooden, rigid-frame construction with nailed plywood gussets. It is about 23 feet wide and the length may be varied as desired. If it is to be covered with plastic film, 48- or 96-foot building lengths are suggested so that unbroken lengths of the film can be applied with a minimum of waste. Access is through 7-foot-square doorways at each end of the building.

The rigid frames are erected on a foundation consisting of short poles set in the ground to support a built-up wood sill assembly. The poles and sill planks should be pressure treated with a nontoxic preservative. Do not use a preservative that may be toxic to plants.

Careful workmanship in cutting and assembling will produce a sturdy frame. As with other light structures, the framing should be securely anchored to the foundation to reduce possible wind damage. For this same reason, the legs of each rigid frame should be fastened to the sill plate with commercial metal framing anchors. All wood above grade should be painted white to reflect a maximum of light.

The initial cost can be reduced by covering the house with plastic film for a season or two and later applying rigid plastic panels for a longer lasting covering. In either case, it is important to follow the manufacturer's directions for installing the plastic.

Exhaust fans installed at one end of the building and air-intake louvers at the other end provide ventilation. Specific ventilation recommendations depend on the size of greenhouse, the type of covering, and the climate of the area in which the house is to be built. Consult your county agricultural agent or State extension agricultural engineer. The air-intake louvers should provide a minimum of 1 square foot of free area for every 1,000 cubic feet per minute of the required fan capacity.

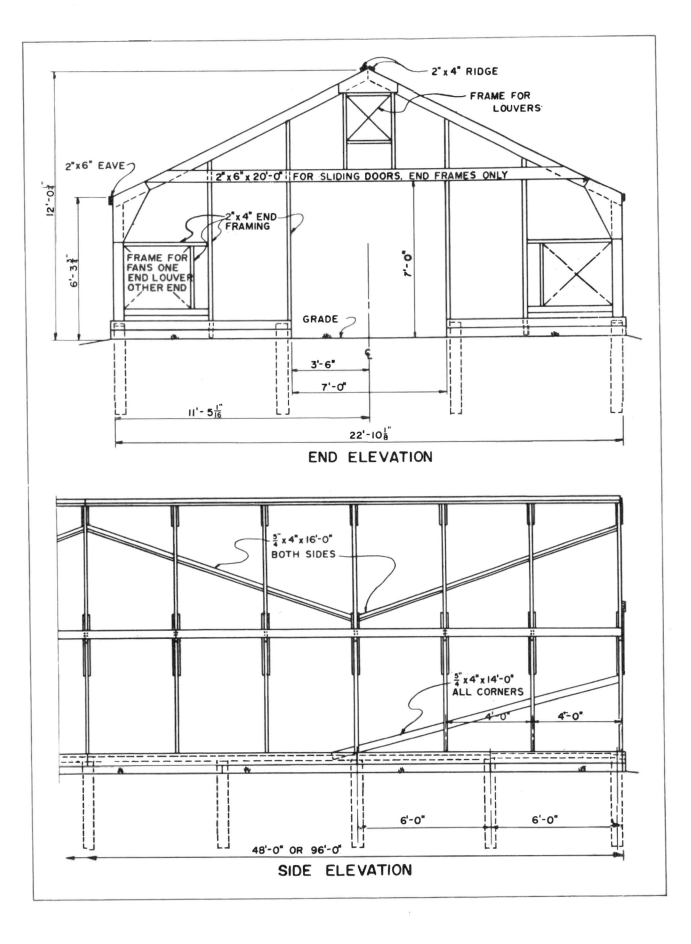

2" x 4" RIDGE

FRAME FOR LOUVERS

2" x 6" EAVE

2" x 6" x 20'-0" FOR SLIDING DOORS, END FRAMES ONLY

2" x 4" END FRAMING

FRAME FOR FANS ONE END LOUVER OTHER END

12'-0"

6'-3¾"

7'-0"

GRADE

3'-6"

7'-0"

11'-5¹⁄₁₆"

22'-10¹⁄₈"

END ELEVATION

¾" x 4" x 16'-0" BOTH SIDES

¾" x 4" x 14'-0" ALL CORNERS

4'-0"

4'-0"

6'-0"

6'-0"

48'-0" OR 96'-0"

SIDE ELEVATION

# HOTBED AND PROPAGATING FRAME, PLAN NO. 5971

This plastic-covered hotbed, which can also be used as a propagating frame, is inexpensive and easy to build.

The hotbed has welded wire frames with removable covers of 4-mil polyethylene plastic film on each side of the ridge. The covers may be rolled down from the ridge or up from the sides to provide almost unlimited adjustment for ventilation. The covers are secured in the desired position with light ropes that pass over the sides and down to the base at each end of the frame. Rubber tubing can be attached at one end of each rope to provide tension. When the spring season is over, the covers can be rolled up and stored out of sunlight to prevent deterioration from ultra-violet radiation. The plastic film that covers the end sections of the structure is not removable, so a long-lasting plastic such as 4-mil vinyl or 3-mil type W polyester film is recommended. Details for making the removable covers are given in the working drawings.

The hotbed is made of wood. It has three arch frames of thin-wall electrical conduit. The frames may be easily bent to shape with a hand conduit bender. The wooden parts should be treated with a preservative after they have been cut. A thorough soaking in a 5-percent solution of pentachlorophenol is suggested.

A soaking trough for treating the wood can be improvised by lining a small trench with polyethylene film. Weight the boards to be sure they are completely immersed in the liquid. Place thin spacers between the boards so the preservative will flow completely around each piece.

**Precaution:** Keep children and animals away from the soaking trough. Follow directions given on the label for use of the preservative.

The hotbed should be located on well-drained soil. Some locations may require a 3-inch layer of gravel under the prepared soil mixture or flats. For supplementary heating, a 360-watt electric soil-heating cable

# HOTBED & PROPAGATING FRAME

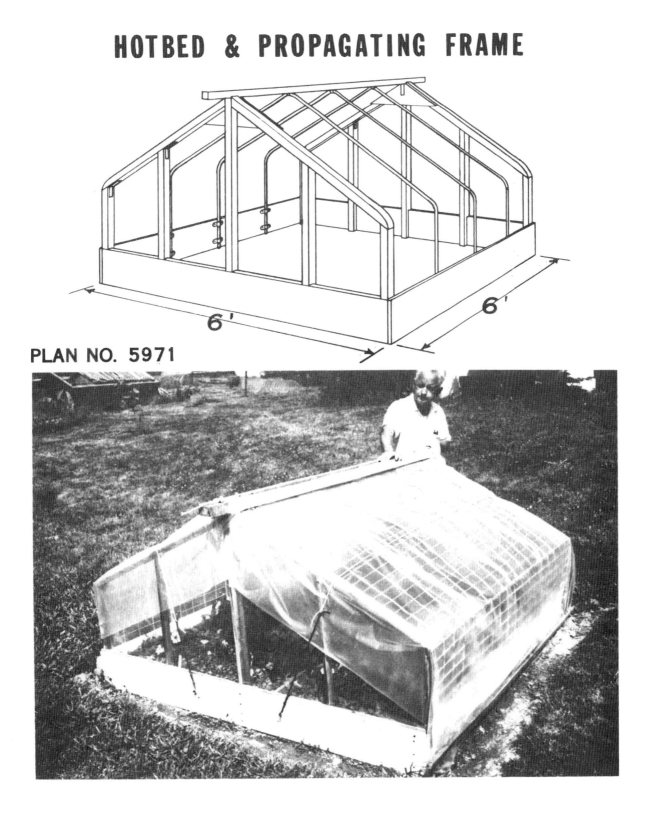

PLAN NO. 5971

55

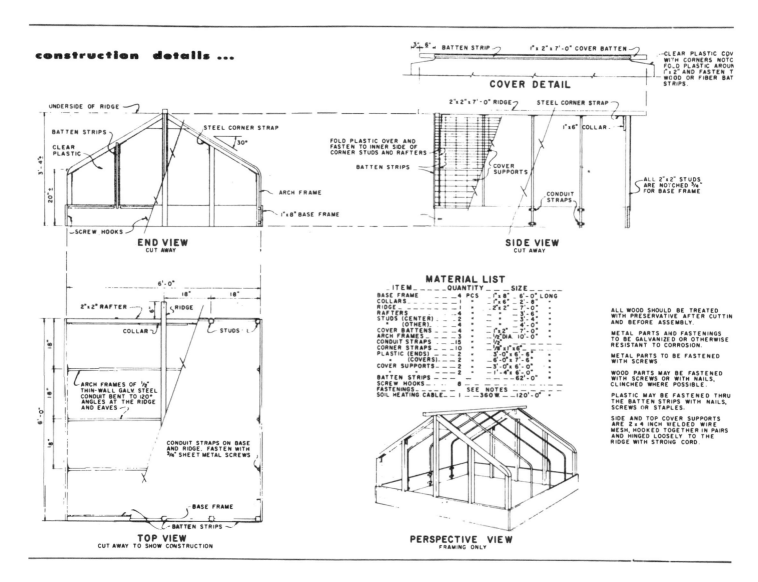

with a 70° thermostat is suggested. The cable is laid on a bed of sand or vermiculite and covered with about 2 inches of sand. If the seed or cuttings are to be started in a prepared soilbed rather than in pots or flats, the cable is protected by placing ½-inch-mesh hardware cloth about 1-inch above it.

## The propagating frame

When the hotbed is used as a propagating frame, the welded wire frame is covered with cheesecloth fastened with clothespins. Two mist sprayers, fastened to a 2 by 2 board 8 feet long, can be mounted quickly and easily on the inside of the frame, diagonally and about 1 foot above the cuttings, or on the outside above the ridge. The location of the sprayers depends on the weather. If it is dry and windy, the sprayers are mounted inside. If humid and calm, the sprayers are mounted on the ridge. The frame is kept covered with cheesecloth, and the cheesecloth is moistened several times a day when necessary.

# MINI-HOTBED AND PROPAGATING FRAME, PLAN NO.6080

This plastic-covered hotbed is inexpensive and easy to construct. It is portable and suitable for use in the home backyard.

A 160-watt soil heating cable, thermostatically controlled to shut off at 70° F. is used to heat the structure.

Two pieces of plastic film that cover the frame overlap at the top and are held taut with snap clothespins. Plastic webbing permits closing up the hotbed at night.

Ventilation is achieved during the day by pulling down the plastic film from the top and fastening it with clothespins.

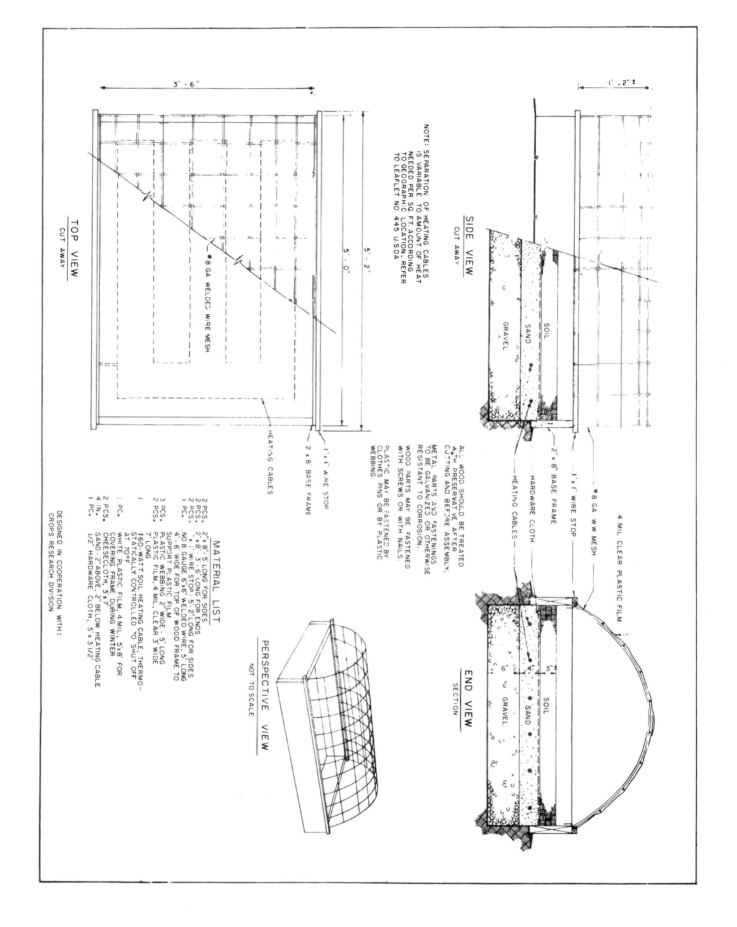

**TOP VIEW**
CUT AWAY

3' - 6"

5' - 0"

5' - 2"

#8 GA WELDED WIRE MESH

HEATING CABLES

1" x 1" WIRE STOP

2 x 8' BASE FRAME

NOTE: SEPARATION OF HEATING CABLES IS VARIABLE TO AMOUNT OF HEAT NEEDED PER SQ. FT. ACCORDING TO GEOGRAPHIC LOCATION. REFER TO LEAFLET NO. 445 USDA.

**SIDE VIEW**
CUT AWAY

1' - 2" ±

GRAVEL

SAND

SOIL

**END VIEW**
SECTION

4 MIL CLEAR PLASTIC FILM

#8 GA WW MESH

1" x 1" WIRE STOP

2" x 8" BASE FRAME

HARDWARE CLOTH

HEATING CABLES

6"

4"

3"

GRAVEL

SOIL

SAND

METAL PARTS AND FASTENINGS TO BE GALVANIZED OR OTHERWISE RESISTANT TO CORROSION.

WOOD PARTS MAY BE FASTENED WITH SCREWS OR WITH NAILS.

PLASTIC MAY BE FASTENED BY CLOTHES PINS OR BY PLASTIC WEBBING.

ALL WOOD SHOULD BE TREATED WITH PRESERVATIVE AFTER CUTTING AND BEFORE ASSEMBLY.

**PERSPECTIVE VIEW**
NOT TO SCALE

**MATERIAL LIST**

2 PCS. 2" x 8" - 5' LONG FOR SIDES
2 PCS. 2" x 8" - 3' - 6" LONG FOR ENDS
2 PCS. 1" x 1" WIRE STOP - 5' LONG FOR SIDES
1 PC. NO 8 GAUGE 6"x 6" WELDED WIRE, 5' LONG
4', 6" WIDE FOR TOP OF WOOD FRAME TO SUPPORT PLASTIC FILM
3 PCS. PLASTIC WEBBING, 2" WIDE - 5' LONG
2 PCS. PLASTIC FILM, 4 MIL, CLEAR 3' WIDE 7' LONG
1 160-WATT SOIL HEATING CABLE, THERMO-STATICALLY CONTROLLED TO SHUT OFF AT 70°F
1 PC. WHITE PLASTIC FILM, 4 MIL, 5'x 8' FOR COVERING FRAME DURING WINTER
2 PCS. CHEESECLOTH, 3'x 7'
4 IN. SAND - 2" ABOVE, 2" BELOW HEATING CABLE
1 PC. 1/2" HARDWARE CLOTH, 5 x 3 1/2'

DESIGNED IN COOPERATION WITH:
CROPS RESEARCH DIVISION

58

# RECREATIONAL FACILITIES

## OUTDOOR FIREPLACE, PLAN NO. 5188

In recent years, structures that can be used either as a small barbeque pit or simply for outdoor cooking have become quite popular. Therefore, the trend in barbeque pits is for a structure somewhat like the one illustrated.

The fireplace and grill shown are large enough for cooking meals for 10 to 20 persons; it can also be used as a trash burner.

Consult your local authorities on environmental control before starting construction of this fireplace.

# Construction details

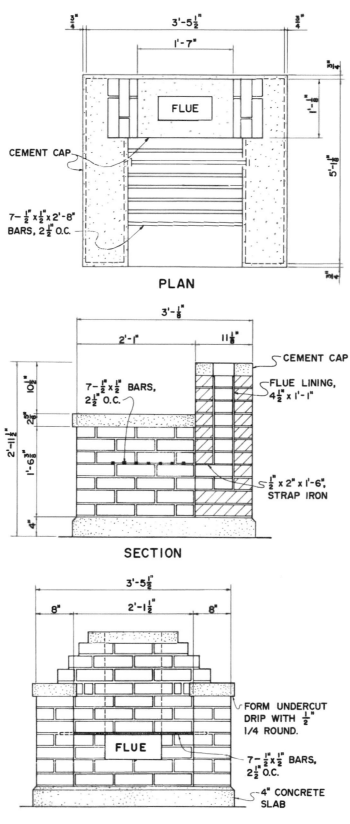

PLAN

SECTION

FRONT VIEW

CEMENT CAP

FLUE

7—$\frac{1}{2}$" x $\frac{1}{2}$" x 2'-8"
BARS, 2$\frac{1}{2}$" O.C.

3'-5$\frac{1}{2}$"

1'-7"

3$\frac{3}{4}$"

3$\frac{3}{4}$"

1'-1$\frac{5}{8}$"

5'-1$\frac{5}{8}$"

3'-1$\frac{1}{8}$"

2'-1"

11$\frac{1}{8}$"

CEMENT CAP

FLUE LINING,
4$\frac{1}{2}$" x 1'-1"

7—$\frac{1}{2}$" x $\frac{1}{2}$" BARS,
2$\frac{1}{2}$" O.C.

$\frac{1}{2}$" x 2" x 1'-6",
STRAP IRON

10$\frac{1}{2}$"

2$\frac{5}{8}$"

2'-11$\frac{1}{2}$"

1'-6$\frac{3}{8}$"

4"

3'-5$\frac{1}{2}$"

8"

2'-1$\frac{1}{2}$"

8"

FLUE

FORM UNDERCUT
DRIP WITH $\frac{1}{2}$"
1/4 ROUND.

7—$\frac{1}{2}$" x $\frac{1}{2}$" BARS,
2$\frac{1}{2}$" O.C.

4" CONCRETE
SLAB

# BOAT LANDING, PLAN NO. 5975

Summer is a good time to build a boat landing. This all-weather dock for a small boat is designed for use in a sound where waves do not exceed 3 feet and the tide is normally 2 to 3 feet. Although it is built to withstand winds of hurricane force, the dock is not suitable for a river or lake where massive ice floes can cause structural damage.

Any location on an open stretch of water is subjected to higher winds than an inland site. Therefore, build this shelter extra strong to resist wind forces. Fasten the roof down well. Drive at least four deformed-shank, 9-gage (diameter, 0.144 inch), galvanized roofing nails, 2 inches long, into each sheet at each purlin (the 2- by 8-inch members that support the roof lengthwise). At least 4 pounds of nails this size are required to anchor the roof. Spike the purlins securely to 2- by 8-inch purlin ties and, in turn, spike the purlin ties to both 2- by 8-inch rafters. Bolt the rafters to the pilings.

Well-anchored pilings are necessary to keep the building intact. In most areas the pilings can be set without special equipment. A water jet will penetrate ordinary clays. Pressure and volume of water required for jetting a pile hole vary with the depth of waterhead above the jet and with the density and tightness of the clay. An ordinary garden hose, equipped with a nozzle and fed from a domestic water system (shallow well pump, driven by a ½-horsepower electrical motor) has been used successfully for pile setting.

Jetting a pilot hole about 3 or 4 inches in diameter is done by fastening the garden hose and nozzle to a steel bar (crowbar) about 6 feet long, and approximately 1 inch square. The end of the bar should be chisel- or diamond-pointed and tempered to hold the point. Fasten the nozzle of the hose 2 inches above the point, to deliver a jet stream to the point. Drive a hole in the bottom by plunging the steel bar and hose up and down. Do not be disturbed if the pilot hole fills with sand when you remove the jet; the hole serves as a soft spot to guide the piling in a vertical position. Insert a pointed piling in the top of the pilot hole; with the garden hose on either a stick or a steel bar, continue jetting beneath the pile by plunging the jet nozzle down and up.

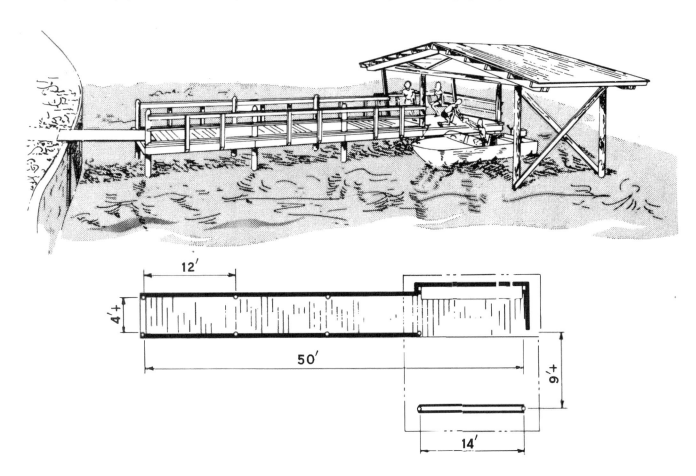

Moving the jet up and down produces a drawing action on the pile; the pile may also be slightly lifted and dropped to increase the movement of slush to the soil material under the pile.

Set the pile at least 5 feet deep to give good bottom anchorage to the boathouse. Piles for the wharf may be set shallower—3 to 4 feet. The greatest force exerted on a wharf comes from driving waves. A low wharf is more convenient than a high wharf, but driving waves will knock the decking from a low wharf unless the decking has better anchorage than that provided by nails through the deck into the stringers.

The design shows a 2 by 4 toe guard along the outside edges on top of the decking. This guard is fastened by an eyebolt (5/16 inch in diameter and 8 inches long) through the toe guard and the deck. The eye of the bolt lies beside the 2- by 8-inch stringer. A bolt, 5/16 inch in diameter, with large washers ties the

eyebolt to the stringer; the stringer is securely bolted to the piling with a bolt ½ inch in diameter.

The gangplank between the wharf and the shoreline should not be rigidly fastened to the wharf because the free-moving piles of the structure adjust their positions to resist water and wind (one secret of piling strength). The gangplank can be rigidly fastened on the shore and can rest freely on the wharf.

When left in the landing shed unattended, the boat should be raised out of the water. A steel cable (1/8 inch to 3/16 inch in diameter) attached to winches on the piles at each end of the boathouse can be attached to a block hung from the rafters. If the cable passing through the block is strung between the lower rafter ties on the pathway to the fall, the wind and waves cannot swing the boat enough for it to strike the piles. Fore and aft slings made of webbing can be looped under the boat. Spreader sticks, made from 2- by 3-inch clear lumber, may be placed in the slings above the gunwales to prevent the slings from pulling the gunwales inward. Spreader sticks will not be needed on well-built boats. The fore sling can be dropped over the bow, but the aft sling may have to be placed beneath the boat in front of the propeller if an outboard motor is used. If the sling has to go beneath instead of looping over the stern, the task can be made easier by installing a quick-acting snap in the sling and by stiffening the sling with a piece of material cut from an old automobile tire. The stiffened sling can be more easily inserted beneath the boat.

A locker and seat, installed on the landing dock, may be used to keep oars, gasoline, skis, fishing tackle, life preservers, and similar equipment needed for your safe enjoyment of the water.

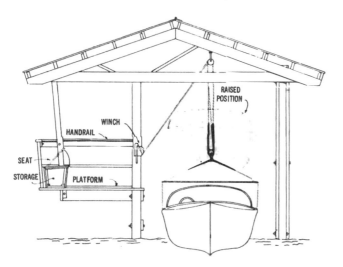

## PICNIC SHELTER OF WOOD CONSTRUCTION, PLAN NO. 5995

Economy of construction and distinctive architectural design make this picnic shelter a unique attraction and landmark for a recreational area.

The roof is especially stable because its long, projecting overhang at the three points of a triangle provides a counterbalance for the high crown. This counterbalancing force eliminates much of the horizontal thrust on the top of the posts. Because thrust is rather negligible, the posts have no tension ties but, instead, are stabilized by concrete collars at the ground surface.

The shelter is designed as a roof, consisting of three doubly warped surfaces supported by three wooden posts, 20 feet apart. The roof covers an equilateral triangular area of 693 square feet. Each side is 40 feet long. These doubly warped surfaces are known as hyperbolic paraboloids.

Each of the three surfaces is made by two sets of crossing straight lines that join two opposite edge members (see 1-unit plan view). In construction, these lines are actually formed by two layers of ¼- by 12-inch hardboard strips that cross each other and are nailed at

PLAN VIEW

0  5  10  15
SCALE IN FEET

their ends to 2- by 8-inch edge members. To achieve warping without sagging of the strips, temporary 2- by 4-inch rafters are fastened at quarter points on two opposite edge members.

Before the second layer of strips is laid, the first layer is covered with fiberglass fabric to bridge the gap between strips. After the fabric is in place, the two layers of strips are then bolted together with at least two 5/16-inch carriage bolts at each intersection. When bolting is finished, the strips are end trimmed, ridges are covered with roll material, and the overhang is bound with formed angle of sheet metal. The surface thus formed is ready to be weatherproofed by mopping two coats of stabilized asphalt with a three-knot roofing brush. Additional fiberglass fabric is used to bridge gaps wherever needed. This procedure applies to all roof surfaces. Rafters and scaffolding can be used again.

The asphalt roof coating provides weather protection for about 2 years. At the end of this time, the roof should be remopped to prevent the occurrence of pin holes between the intersections of the hardboard strips.

As shown below in the plan view of a 6-unit layout, additional triangular roof units can be joined to provide a larger shelter. The technique of joining triangular units is made practical by using a 5-inch pipe column instead of a wooden post for interior support. This pipe column then becomes a storm drain through which one-third of the roof water flows to a disposal line installed under the building. Six of these roof units can be joined together to form a hexagonal type of building supported by six wooden posts and six pipe columns, which serve as storm drains for two-thirds of roof water. Since this is a new type of fabrication to which workmen are not accustomed, the cost of fabrication will be higher than the cost of material.

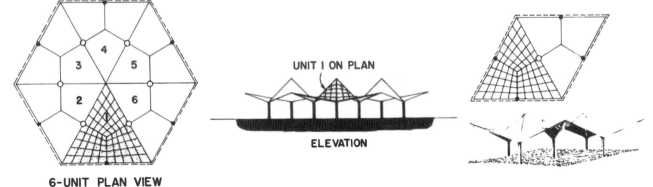

6-UNIT PLAN VIEW

UNIT I ON PLAN

ELEVATION

# CONCRETE BLOCK INCINERATOR, PLAN NO. 5996

Engineers at the University of Connecticut designed this oil-fired incinerator. It is capable of burning a variety of material—trash, garbage, dead poultry, or any other combustible refuse that is small enough to be placed in the incinerator basket. Incineration of dead birds and similar material may cause a bad odor. This can be alleviated by heating the firebrick in the combustion chamber before placing the material to be burned in it. This helps the burning of the volatile gases and eliminates most of the odor.

Garbage should be drained and wrapped in paper before placing it in the steel basket for burning. The steel basket can be taken from the incinerator so that tin cans and other incombustible material mixed with the garbage can be removed. Heat of incineration destroys all disease organisms, making this method of trash disposal desirable and relatively inexpensive.

The incinerator should be operated only when it can be attended and supervised by a responsible person. An attendant is needed to see that incineration consumes all the combustible material, that the area is kept sanitary, and that sparks do not cause unwanted fire.

Incineration is one method of disposing of garbage accumulated in picnic areas. This can be done during inspections when tables are scrubbed and litter and garbage are removed.

Consult State and local authorities to insure compliance with health and building requirements and to avoid possible environmental pollution.

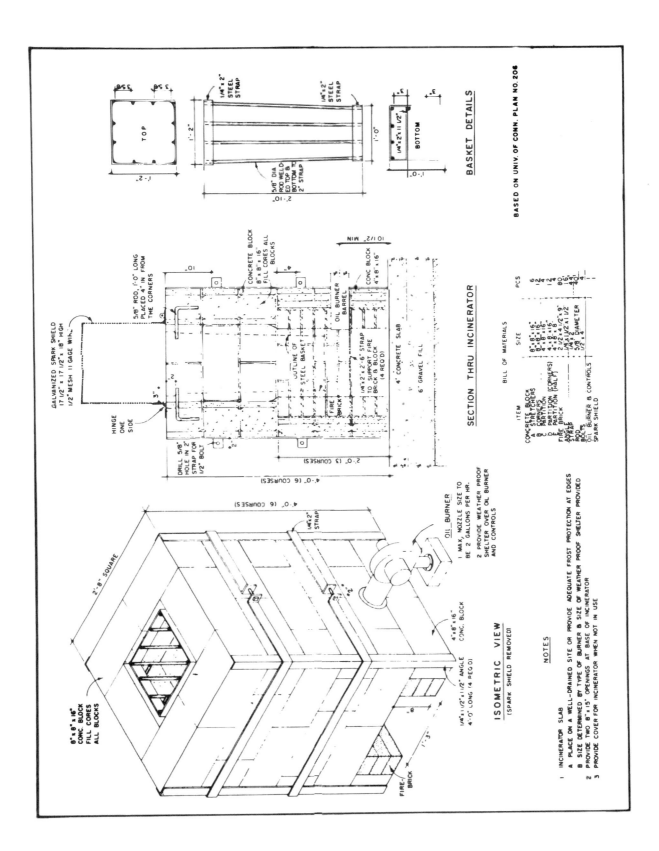

BASKET DETAILS

BASED ON UNIV. OF CONN. PLAN NO. 206

SECTION THRU INCINERATOR

ISOMETRIC VIEW
(SPARK SHIELD REMOVED)

OIL BURNER

1 MAX. NOZZLE SIZE TO
BE 2 GALLONS PER HR.
2 PROVIDE WEATHER PROOF
SHELTER OVER OIL BURNER
AND CONTROLS

BILL OF MATERIALS

| ITEM | SIZE | PCS |
|---|---|---|
| CONCRETE BLOCK | 8"x8"x16" | 6 |
| A CORNERS | 8"x8"x16" | 12 |
| B CORNERS | 4"x8"x16" | 4 |
| C PARTITION | 4"x8"x16" | 4 |
| D PARTITION (CORNERS) | 2 1/2"x4"x8" | 9 |
| E PARTITION (HALF) | | |
| FIRE BRICK | 4 1/2"x4 1/2"x9" | 80 |
| ANGLE | 1/4"x1 1/2"x1 1/2 | 4 |
| STRAP | 1/4"x2 | 16 |
| ROD | 5/8" DIAMETER | 4 |
| BOLT | 1/2"x4 | 4 |
| OIL BURNER & CONTROLS | | 1 |
| SPARK SHIELD | | 1 |

NOTES

1 INCINERATOR SLAB
   A PLACE ON A WELL-DRAINED SITE OR PROVIDE ADEQUATE FROST PROTECTION AT EDGES
   B SIZE DETERMINED BY TYPE OF BURNER B SIZE OF WEATHER PROOF SHELTER PROVIDED
2 PROVIDE TWO 8"x15" OPENINGS AT BASE OF INCINERATOR
3 PROVIDE COVER FOR INCINERATOR WHEN NOT IN USE

65

# SHELTERED BARBEQUE PITS, PLANS NO. 6020 AND NO. 6022

NO. 6020

In many areas, barbeques pits are very popular and can be used to cook large quantities of meat at one time when necessary. These plans for building sheltered barbeque pits were developed in response to requests from many organizations such as cattlemen's associations, poultrymen's associations, and other farm groups.

The pit described here can be built in increments of 5 feet so that a pit from 5 to 30 feet can be easily constructed.

Metal doors at either end of the pit give convenient access to the firebox.

Because some meats should be cooked slowly and others more rapidly, the plans include an adjustable grill.

In Plan 6022, the end- and sidewalls of the shelter are screened to keep out insects. A screen door at each end of the structure provides convenient access to the pit. The concrete slab and the roof extend past both ends of the pit to permit free movement around the entire pit.

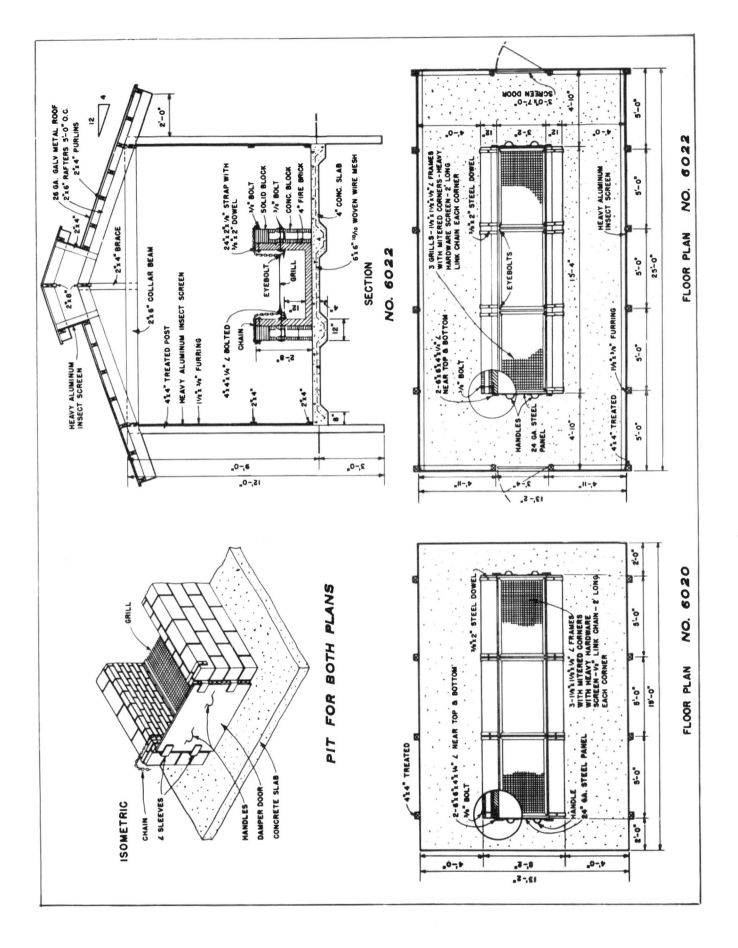

26 GA. GALV METAL ROOF
2"x6" RAFTERS 5'-0" O.C.
2"x4" PURLINS

12

2'-0"

2"x4"

2"x8"

2"x4" COLLAR BEAM

2"x4" BRACE

HEAVY ALUMINUM INSECT SCREEN

4"x4" TREATED POST
HEAVY ALUMINUM INSECT SCREEN
1½"x½" FURRING

2½"x2½x½" STRAP WITH ½"x12" DOWEL

¼" BOLT
SOLID BLOCK
½" BOLT
CONC. BLOCK
4" FIRE BRICK
4" CONC. SLAB

6"x6" ¹⁰⁄₁₀ WOVEN WIRE MESH

EYEBOLT
GRILL
CHAIN

4¼"x4¼x¼" L BOLTED
2"x4"
2"x4"

2'-0"

12"

9'-0"
12'-0"
3'-0"

SECTION
NO. 6022

3'-0"x7'-0"
SCREEN DOOR

4'-10"

4'-0"
12"
3'-2"
12"
4'-0"

5'-0"

5'-0"

5'-0"

5'-0"

25'-0"

3 GRILLS–1½"x1½x1½" L FRAMES WITH MITERED CORNERS – HEAVY HARDWARE SCREEN – 2' LONG LINK CHAIN EACH CORNER

15'-4"

⅜"x12" STEEL DOWEL

EYEBOLTS

2–6"x6"x¼" L NEAR TOP & BOTTOM

¼" BOLT

HANDLES
24 GA STEEL PANEL

4'-10"

HEAVY ALUMINUM INSECT SCREEN

1½"x½" FURRING

4"x4" TREATED

5'-0"

FLOOR PLAN    NO. 6022

4'-11"
3'-4"
4'-11"
13'-2"

GRILL

ISOMETRIC

CHAIN
4 SLEEVES

HANDLES
DAMPER DOOR
CONCRETE SLAB

PIT FOR BOTH PLANS

⅜"x12" STEEL DOWEL

3–1½"x1½x½" L FRAMES WITH MITERED CORNERS WITH HEAVY HARDWARE SCREEN – ½" LINK CHAIN – 2' LONG EACH CORNER

2–6"x6"x¼" L NEAR TOP & BOTTOM

¼" BOLT

HANDLE
24 GA. STEEL PANEL

4"x4" TREATED

2'-0"

5'-0"

15'-0"

5'-0"

2'-0"

4'-0"
3'-2"
4'-0"
13'-2"

FLOOR PLAN    NO. 6020

67

# RECREATIONAL PAVILION WITH KITCHEN, PLAN NO. 6079

This recreational pavilion with kitchen was designed at Cornell University to meet an increasing need in parks and other recreational areas in New York State. It could be used in any part of the United States except in areas where snow accumulations may be extremely heavy. The pavilion has facilities for preparing and serving food and may be easily enclosed for all-year, all-weather use. The working drawings include an alternate floor plan for extending the kitchen the full width of the pavilion and for adding a fireplace.

For sanitation, the floor in the kitchen is of concrete, and the designers suggest that some type of paving also be used on the rest of the covered area. According to the effect desired, this paving could be brick, flagstone, treated woodblock, or other durable and reasonably flat material. The paving should extend an additional 3 feet on all sides of the pavilion.

The building may be lengthened in 12-foot units. The siding may be applied either horizontally or vertically and stained or painted to harmonize or contrast with the surroundings.

The pavilion is of pole construction, with clear span trusses supporting the roof. The working drawings include details for building these trusses, which are designed to support roof loads up to 30 pounds per square foot. If desired, commercially fabricated trusses could be substituted, with the result of a reduction in cost of onsite labor.

**NOTE:** As a protection for clothing, the poles should be pressure treated with a nonstaining preservative.

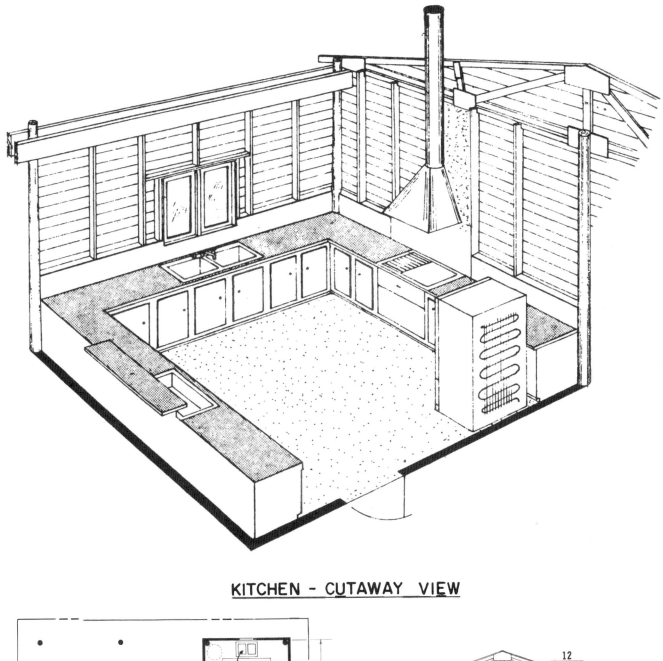

## KITCHEN - CUTAWAY VIEW

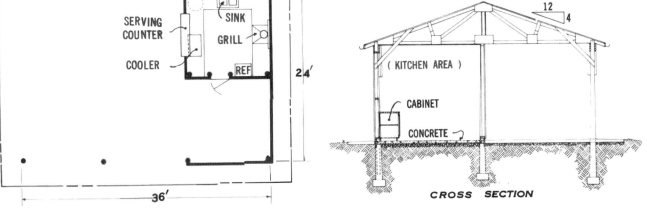

SERVING
COUNTER

COOLER

SINK

GRILL

REF

24'

36'

12
4

( KITCHEN AREA )

CABINET

CONCRETE

CROSS SECTION

# COMFORT STATION FOR CAMPGROUNDS, PLAN NO. 6083

The design for this comfort station was developed at Rutgers University, New Brunswick, N.J., and is based on the operators' code of the New Jersey Private Campground Association. The comfort station is intended to serve 50 campsites—or about 200 people.

To reduce maintenance, the building has no windows. Instead, natural light is admitted through translucent plastic panels that cover the top 2 feet of all four walls. As an alternate, the panels could be installed as skylights in a corrugated metal roof, but it should be noted that in open, unshaded locations, skylights can contribute to an undesirable buildup of heat within the building.

Positive ventilation is provided by a two-speed exhaust fan mounted in one gable end of the building and several screened, floor-level intake vents in the walls.

Consult State and local authorities to insure compliance with health and building requirements and to avoid possible environmental pollution.

**ALTERNATE CONSTRUCTION**

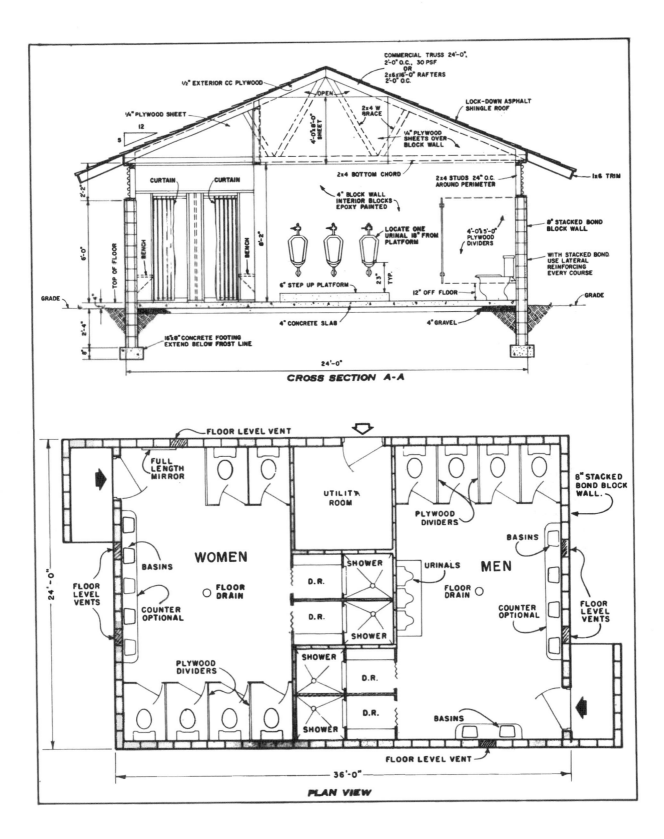

CROSS SECTION A-A

PLAN VIEW

71

# STORAGE SHEDS, PLANS NO. 6086 AND NO. 6093

These two plans offer a choice of five different designs for small sheds which are suitable for a variety of uses, such as:

(1) The storage of lawn and garden tools, equipment, and supplies, patio furniture, sports equipment, bicycles and toys.

(2) A workshop or house for hobbies.

(3) A playhouse or poolside cabana.

(4) A shelter for a small pony.

Plan No. 6093 was developed at Virginia Polytechnic Institute in the style of a traditional gambrel-roofed barn, with the battens painted to contrast with the color of the vertical board siding, such as white over red barn stain.

Plan No. 6086 was developed at Clemson University, Clemson, S.C. The plan shows details of construction for four sheds of more contemporary styling.

All five sheds are of light frame construction, erected on 4-inch thick reinforced concrete floor slabs with thickened edges.

Many exterior materials and finishes may be used, such as real or simulated board-and-batten, textured plywood, and horizontal or vertical siding.

In some localities, building permits are required for structures such as these. Consult authorities before starting construction.

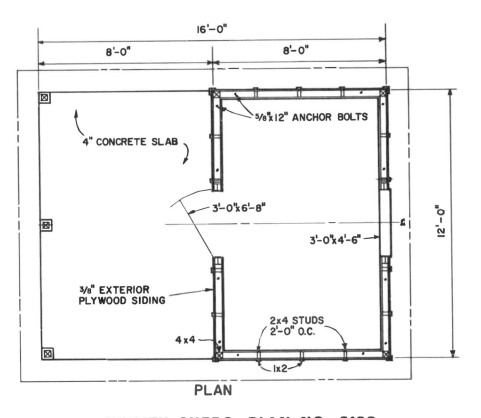

**PLAN**

## UTILITY SHEDS, PLAN NO. 6100

The plan for the utility shed illustrated here was developed at the University of Connecticut, Storrs. The shed is one of many different designs, some of which are shown.

Working drawings for the sheds include a list of materials needed for construction.

The plan is for panel-type construction: The 2-by-4 framing is covered with exterior-type plywood panels and is secured to a 4-inch-thick concrete-floor slab with two anchor bolts per panel.

In some areas, building permits are required for this type structure. Consult your local building authorities before starting construction.

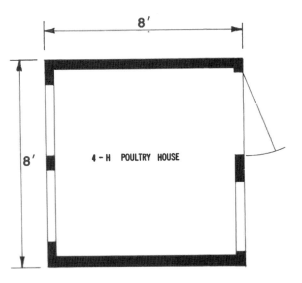

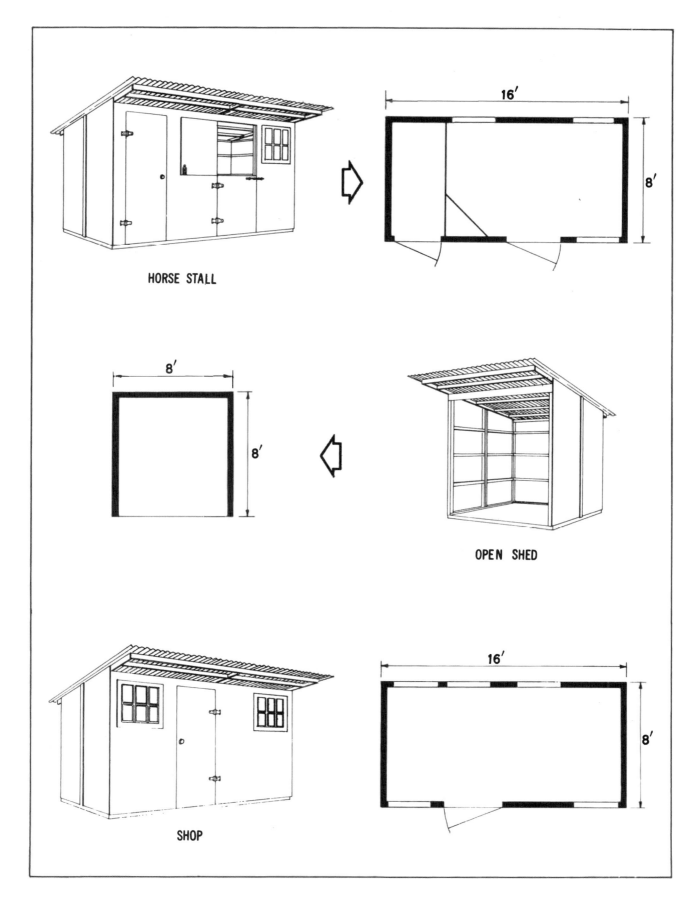

HORSE STALL

16'

8'

8'

8'

OPEN SHED

SHOP

16'

8'